New Directions for
Higher Education

Betsy O. Barefoot
Jillian L. Kinzie
Co-editors

Enhancing Student Learning and Development in Cross-Border Higher Education

Dennis C. Roberts
Susan R. Komives
Editors

Number 175 • Fall 2016
Jossey-Bass
San Francisco

ENHANCING STUDENT LEARNING AND DEVELOPMENT IN CROSS-BORDER HIGHER EDUCATION
Dennis C. Roberts, Susan R. Komives
New Directions for Higher Education, no. 175
Betsy O. Barefoot and Jillian L. Kinzie, Co-editors

Microfilm copies of issues and articles are available in 16mm and 35mm, as well as microfiche in 105mm, through University Microfilms Inc., 300 North Zeeb Road, Ann Arbor, MI 48106-1346.

NEW DIRECTIONS FOR HIGHER EDUCATION (ISSN 0271-0560, electronic ISSN 1536-0741) is part of The Jossey-Bass Higher and Adult Education Series and is published quarterly by Wiley Subscription Services, Inc., A Wiley Company, at Jossey-Bass, One Montgomery Street, Suite 1200, San Francisco, CA 94104-4594. POSTMASTER: Send address changes to New Directions for Higher Education, Jossey-Bass, One Montgomery Street, Suite 1200, San Francisco, CA 94104-4594.

New Directions for Higher Education is indexed in Current Index to Journals in Education (ERIC); Higher Education Abstracts.

Individual subscription rate (in USD): $89 per year US/Can/Mex, $113 rest of world; institutional subscription rate: $335 US, $375 Can/Mex, $409 rest of world. Single copy rate: $29. Electronic only–all regions: $89 individual, $335 institutional; Print & Electronic–US: $98 individual, $402 institutional; Print & Electronic–Canada/Mexico: $98 individual, $442 institutional; Print & Electronic–Rest of World: $122 individual, $476 institutional.

Editorial correspondence should be sent to the Co-editor, Betsy O. Barefoot, Gardner Institute, Box 72, Brevard, NC 28712.

Cover design: Wiley
Cover Images: © Lava 4 images | Shutterstock

www.josseybass.com

CONTENTS

Part Three: Foundations and Strategies

EDITORS' NOTES

The journey of this book started when we decided to couple a short-term study abroad experience for Susan's University of Maryland graduate students and a group from the University of San Diego with the professional development of student affairs staff with whom Denny worked at Qatar Foundation's Education City in Doha. This project, supported and funded by Qatar Foundation, was catalytic in our professional lives. Although we had known each other for many years, the challenge of creating mutually informing and beneficial learning among an extremely diverse group of graduate students and new professionals put our intellects and planning skills to the supreme test when we designed the Qatar Study Tour with culminating Young Professionals Institute in 2010. Cross-sectional groups from all three settings prepared in advance and worked in collaborative teams on topics related to the student experience in Education City. These teams reported their recommendations in a day-long institute for those doing student affairs work in several institutions in Doha. The outcome of the initial experience was so positive that we chose to replicate it for a second time in 2012 and the model continues to be utilized as an ongoing partnership in higher education internationalization. This partnership changed the way we viewed internationalization, and it caused us to begin planning for a book that would invite others to more deeply explore the prospects of cross-border higher education in their work.

Internationalizing Higher Education

Higher education is expanding and changing rapidly around the world. Whole regions of the world, such as the European Union, are collaborating in new ways. Many countries such as China and South Africa are seeking good practices from western universities and adapting them to their context. Many institutions in western and northern countries, such as the United States, Canada, the United Kingdom, and France, are internationalizing and establishing branch programs or campuses around the world.

This volume addresses the opportunities and challenges in developing programs and strategies for student learning and development that are culturally appropriate for those considering adopting best practices from other regions of the world. The volume also advances using the whole institutional environment—educational experiences in the curriculum and

NEW DIRECTIONS FOR HIGHER EDUCATION, no. 175, Fall 2016 © 2016 Wiley Periodicals, Inc.
Published online in Wiley Online Library (wileyonlinelibrary.com) • DOI: 10.1002/he.20193

co-curriculum—to further desired student learning and developmental outcomes.

Much of what is included in this book relates specifically to what western higher education offers through student affairs, student development, and student services. However, concurrently, the student experience in the United States would benefit from examining and adapting practices from other nations, such as the adaptations occurring from the Bologna process or the care-leavers example, those leaving foster care, offered in the United Kingdom that is profiled in this volume.

Using This Volume

Because student affairs as a specialty in higher education is so unique to practice in the United States, many of the broader international higher education community, such as faculty, administrators, policy makers, and funders, are unaware that much of what the United States has achieved in quality higher education derives from the holistic and engaging approach that is advocated by student affairs staff. This volume was written to serve all those who value quality higher education no matter what their role. The intent of this volume was to convince broader constituencies of the merit of enhancing the student experience so that students worldwide will benefit from enhanced learning and development opportunities.

Essential Ideas and Topics in This Volume

The journey of this volume involved careful selection of topics that would be essential to the reader's understanding of student learning and development, and finding authors who had broad exposure to international and cross-border higher education, where some of the most interesting work is taking place.

The chapters in this volume are organized into three sections. The two chapters in the first section set the stage for critically analyzing the cross-cultural application of educational practices outside the countries where they are presently used. We begin by proposing in Chapter 1 that if international educators seek a commensurate impact through higher education to what occurred in the United States in the 20th century, it is critical to know what matters most in providing the highest possible quality experience for students. The chapter proposes that educators should seek the full engagement of learners, like what takes place in the best colleges and universities. The chapter also acknowledges that best practices from the United States and other countries could be transferred in some cases but that in most cases the practices should be modified—adapted, hedged, or even avoided all together. Chapter 2 acknowledges that the motivations of educators involved in internationalization will have a significant impact on what educational practices are chosen or adapted. The "heuristics of diffusion" that drive educators and policy makers will vary across a continuum from learning from others, imitation, conforming to others' norms, competition, and even coercion. Understanding what the motivation is and who influences the decision-making processes related to internationalization impacts not only the focus of any educational initiative but it may also be central to its credibility and sustainability.

Chapters 3 through 6 are clustered in the second section to provide examples of practice designed to enhance student learning and development positioned within the local, regional, or national needs of the institutions represented. Whether the particular practice is relevant to every reader, why the initiative was important, and how it impacted students demonstrates the best of practices in planning for any student learning and development effort. Readers can determine if those programs could be transferred, adapted, or should be avoided in their own national context. The South African example of establishing living communities to support students unprepared for the demands of higher education may be relevant for many institutions that have first-generation or underserved students. By contrast, the example from China proposes an approach to help "indulged" students learn to be more resilient and effective in adverse circumstances. The example from the United Kingdom sheds light on what it takes to foster retention and success for students who were at great risk—those leaving alternative care providers from childhood. The final chapter from Mexico describes the pressing need to cultivate civic and democratic attitudes and skills among young people. These four examples only scratch the surface of the ingenuity and creativity taking place in many international settings, innovation borne of unique needs that serve students, institutions, and multiple stakeholders.

The third section, Chapters 7 through 11, introduces topics that are broadly applicable across all educational, cultural, and national contexts. The approaches and methods described in these five chapters are central to the appropriate cultural modification of educational practices as well as legitimation of higher education institutions. Chapter 7 summarizes the research and theorizes about how students develop a sense of identity and how their cognitive processes become increasingly complex and effective. Chapter 8 describes how students' cultural experiences relate to the environments where they study; this interaction of person and environment is ultimately one of the most important stimuli for learning. Refinement of research, evaluation, and assessment in higher education is the topic of Chapter 9. As Chapters 1 and 2 describe, the specific details of the research and theory in student learning and development, as well as student and community characteristics, will vary across settings. It is, therefore, important that research and new theorizing is undertaken to enhance the new and developing higher-education settings that are now so prominent around the world. Chapter 10 reports findings of a study of educators engaged in student affairs work internationally. The findings indicate a breadth of educational preparation and experience, a strength in many ways but also a challenge in terms of cultivating expertise and advancing higher-quality services and programs. The chapter proposes a number of different staffing strategies that can be used to advance internationalization in higher education. Chapter 11 turns to action and addresses the question "What is to be done?"

Reflecting Again on Our Experience

Returning to the example of our joint project, the Qatar Study Tour and Young Professionals Institute was based on cross-sectional and cross-cultural groups dedicated to mutual learning and focused on enhancing the student experience in Education City. The concluding day-long institute served those doing student affairs work in several institutions in Doha, and it allowed visitors to acquire powerful insights about internationalization of higher education. This impact unfolded from the willingness of Qatar Foundation to embrace an innovative model and to put its full resources behind its implementation. Several things were done intuitively that we now see were critical to this project's success. These factors included preparing the visitors from the United States to be respectful and curious cultural guests, critiquing and using theory and research to inform the mutual work of visitors and educators in Qatar, focusing the key questions of student learning and development in the local context, and using local informants as valued experts on the local environment. The curiosity, openness, questioning of existing scholarship, and genuine commitment to seeking to understand the culture guided our experience. All participants treasured how much we learned from each other. We would hope the same for all cross-border experiences.

Dennis C. Roberts
Susan R. Komives
Editors

DENNIS C. ROBERTS is an independent consultant who works with colleges and universities to enhance their impact in student leadership learning and international understanding. He was associate provost of Hamad bin Khalifa University and assistant vice president for education with the Qatar Foundation from 2007–2014. He is past president of the American College Personnel Association and has authored four books and over 50 book chapters and other articles on student affairs, student learning, and leadership.

SUSAN R. KOMIVES is professor emerita from the student affairs graduate program at the University of Maryland. A past president of the Council for the Advancement of Standards and the American College Personnel Association, she was vice president for student development at two colleges. She is the coauthor or coeditor of a dozen books including the Handbook for Student Services *(1996, 2003), the* Handbook for Student Leadership Development *(2006, 2011), and* Exploring Leadership *(1998, 2007, 2013).*

NEW DIRECTIONS FOR HIGHER EDUCATION • DOI: 10.1002/he

1

Best practices in internationalizing student learning and development require cultural critical analysis before transferring, adapting, hedging, or avoiding existing practices in cross-border applications both in and beyond the classroom.

Internationalizing Student Learning and Development

Dennis C. Roberts, Susan R. Komives

Offering quality higher education is recognized as a pathway to prosperity in both mature and developing countries around the globe. The dynamics and impact of broader educational opportunity and depth that unfolded in the United States in the 20th century may foreshadow how similar dynamics will unfold in the 21st century in different cultural and regional contexts where educational opportunity is now expanding. International higher education leaders must recognize that student learning and developmental outcomes are accomplished through high-level engagement of students in both classroom and beyond the classroom experiences.

The perspective advocated throughout this volume is that higher education is a precious resource, one that must be managed carefully for maximum benefit of all. High-impact higher education can be achieved through expanding opportunity and by infusing international perspectives into students' experience both at home and across borders, but it must be implemented in ways that preserve the uniqueness of each culture and holds student learning and development as its central focus. Especially for countries just beginning to increase access to tertiary or higher education, two questions emerge: (1) How can the investment of governments and families be maximized? and (2) How can students be mobilized to take full advantage of the enhanced opportunity?

This chapter provides an overview of the expansion of higher education across borders and the internationalization that is unfolding in many higher education institutions. It provides frameworks for effective cross-border practices promoting student success through learning and development across diverse contexts with an emphasis on the importance of students engaging university life in ways that blur boundaries and integrate the student experience.

NEW DIRECTIONS FOR HIGHER EDUCATION, no. 175, Fall 2016 © 2016 Wiley Periodicals, Inc.
Published online in Wiley Online Library (wileyonlinelibrary.com) • DOI: 10.1002/he.20194

9

Key Terms

The expansion and internationalization of higher education that will be explained in this volume relies on the following definitions of common terms.

Globalization of Higher Education. Globalization is frequently used in reference to the economic impact of products and services that have spread across the world with fashion, entertainment, and popular products as primary examples. It assumes growing uniformity and sameness as transportation and communication costs drop, products and services globalize, and inequality increases (Stiglitz, 2013).

Internationalization of Higher Education. Internationalization identifies the growing links across nation, culture, and ideology reflecting "the process of integrating an international, intercultural, or global dimension into the purpose, functions, or delivery of postsecondary education." (Knight, 2004, p. 11). Internationalization is different from globalization in that distinct attributes of identity are accorded value, creating "a higher likelihood of protecting unique cultures" that is so important to individual and national identity. Preserving culture can be accomplished "while at the same time serving to embrace the inevitable—a shrinking planet with growing shared reliance on each other" (Roberts, 2015, p. 10). Internationalization can be accomplished through a variety of means (Knight, 2012) such as curriculum and academic programs, teaching/learning processes, research and scholarly activity, cocurricular activities, extracurricular activities, and liaison with local community based cultural/ethnic groups.

Cross-Border Education. Knight (2012) views one type of internationalization as cross-border education referring to a variety of educational strategies that move across national or regional lines and include *people* (study abroad, degrees, field work, internships, sabbaticals, consulting), *programs* (twinning, franchising, articulating, joint/double degrees, online/distance), *providers* (branch campuses, virtual, merger/acquisition, independent), *projects* (research, curriculum, capacity building, educational services), and *policies* (quality assurance, degree levels, credit accumulation and transfer, and academic mobility).

So globalization reflects a growing similarity and presence of a product or idea in many places around the globe and internationalization is a process of infusing international ideas across a variety of functions and experiences. The distinctions made in these definitions are important because they reflect both different purposes and processes that are often not differentiated when educators talk or write about their work.

Historical Context

As higher education opportunity expanded in the early 20th century in the United States, it was no surprise that, as educators began to recognize the emerging complexities that they faced, they began to devise practices to ensure that the quality of students' experience was maintained at the highest possible level. Shifts in educational philosophy and changes in social dynamics reinforced the importance of deeper and more holistic learning among students that valued both the academic and experiential dimensions of their learning: these pedagogies came to be known as the curriculum and co-curriculum. Enhanced educational opportunity has been recognized as one of the conditions most responsible for the improved economy and quality of life experienced in the United States in the 20th century and studies of developing countries in the 21st century confirm similar outcomes (Oketch, McCowan, & Schendel, 2014).

Deeper student engagement and its impact on graduates remain two of the distinguishing attributes of higher education in the United States. The role of engagement in the entire university experience is well documented (Kuh, 2008; Kuh, Kinzie, Schuh, & Whitt, 2005; Pascarella & Terenzini, 2005). Indeed, paralleling a National Survey of Student Engagement (NSSE) finding, a recent Gallup/Purdue University (2014) alumni study found that "where graduates went to college—public or private, small or large, very selective or not selective—hardly matters at all to their current well-being and their work lives in comparison to their experience in college" (p. 6). The report went on to assert that "When it comes to finding the secret to success, it's not 'where you go,' it's 'how you do it' that makes all the difference" (p. 6).

Expanding Higher Education Opportunity Around the World

Although many countries have long had higher education institutions, a new dynamic of west-to-east and north-to-south geographic transfer has occurred that has focused on students' learning and development. Singapore is an example of this recent refinement in focus of educational goals (discussed further in Chapter 8).

> As a small, young nation, Singapore recognized early that its people were its greatest asset, and investment in education was key to its success in a global economy ... Singapore's higher education policy is now focusing both on improving undergraduate education and creating lifelong learning opportunities. (Duderstadt, Taggart, & Weber, 2008, p. 282)

Thoughtfully adapting practices from the north and west has helped developing countries forefront higher education as an economic and social resource in nation building.

This adaptive process, however, has not always been as thoughtful as it could have been. As north and west institutions have internationalized through such practices as international branch campuses, they have frequently assumed that home practices are equally appropriate in the more culturally diverse regions, often leading to unsustainable change. As Duderstadt et al. (2008) noted:

NEW DIRECTIONS FOR HIGHER EDUCATION • DOI: 10.1002/he

> If the interest, or indeed the obligation, of mature universities in the developed world towards the developing world is to assist in development, rather than simply to exploit a market, then certain principles should be accepted: universities should accept a fundamental purpose as enlarging human freedom; ... mature universities should have the goal of building the capacity of universities in the developing countries; and the quality standards for education transmitted to developing countries should not be inferior to those of developed countries. (pp. 288–289)

A problem with the west to east and north to south transfer is that it is often shaped by an imbalance of power. Frequently, the west/north has what the east/south wants, allowing the west/north to exploit the growing economic strength in the east/south as a way to buoy the west/north's economies and infrastructures. This educational transfer then becomes a commodity of trade, placing a great deal of responsibility on the west/north not to abuse its temporary advantage by offering its help at a high price and without critical examination or adaptation of existing programs and practices.

Emerging International Guidelines.   A variety of international documents advocate that higher education institutions should utilize culturally sensitive practices when pursuing cross-border opportunities or internationalization strategies. Principle 13 in the 2012 International Association of Universities statement on internationalization states:

> The prevailing context for higher education internationalization ... requires all institutions to revisit and affirm internationalization's underlying values, principles, and goals, including but not limited to: intercultural learning; inter-institutional cooperation; mutual benefit; solidarity; mutual respect; and fair partnership. ... It requires institutions everywhere to act as responsible global citizens, committed to help shape a global system of higher education that values academic integrity, quality, equitable access, and reciprocity. (p. 4)

The United States American Council on Education's (ACE) Center for Internationalization and Global Engagement (CIGE) that coordinates a variety of initiatives to assist its member institutions as they internationalize their campuses indicates, "We believe effective internationalization goes beyond traditional study-abroad programs and international student enrollment. It requires a comprehensive institutional commitment that also includes curriculum, research, faculty development, and active strategies for institutional engagement" (ACE, 2014, About CIGE). Such statements are beginning to address the conditions and advocate the processes by which balanced and respectful relationships can be established.

Bias in the Current Concepts.   Higher education literature is often written by those from western perspectives, resulting in the inadvertent and

NEW DIRECTIONS FOR HIGHER EDUCATION • DOI: 10.1002/he

largely unexamined privileging of western perspectives and ideas (Tight, 2014). For example, offering academic programs in another country setting or internationalization of the home campus is sometimes conceived and advocated as the "global reach" of the university. Or, western educational approaches may not recognize the complexity of students' cultural backgrounds, an example being the greater importance of family in students' choice of academic majors and careers in some cultures and contexts. Other examples include coeducation residences and some activities and sports that may not be culturally acceptable at all in some environments. Indeed, those institutions expanding their programs to other countries have sometimes brought dimensions of the student experience without critical examination, often resulting in those practices being culturally irrelevant and ineffective in the host countries.

Strategies for Cross-Border Internationalization

The importance of carefully considering educational practices instead of simply benchmarking and applying a practice cannot be overstated; choices about what to do and how to do it must be based on institutional purposes and values.

Wilkins and Huisman (2012) proposed a model for use in planning branch campuses in various regions of the world, which has promise in other forms of internationalization as well. They indicate that cross-border initiatives should be assessed considering both the cultural distance between the donor and host environment, and the institutional commitment and supports available at the host site(s). After assessing the cultural distance as either high or low, then assessing the certainty of institutional commitments and supports that could result in success and sustainability, decision makers can determine the approach that would have the greatest likelihood of success (see Figure 1.1).

The only situation in which a practice could simply be applied or transferred from one setting to another is when the cultural distance is low and the institutional commitments and supports are high. An example could be adopting an educational practice in a partnership between Canadian and Australian institutions. The most typical circumstance to encounter is one in which the cultural distance may be significant but the commitments and supports predict reasonably achievable success. Adapting practices would then be used when utilizing a practice from a United States institution in Africa when the institutional leadership and resources have been secured to provide a firm foundation for success. Even an environment of low cultural distance can be difficult if commitments and supports are not secured, justifying a strategy of hedging one's bets by seeking other significant linkages or partnerships. The most volatile scenario for internationalization is where the cultural gap is wide and the institutional commitments and supports are low; under these circumstances, avoidance may be the best option.

Figure 1.1. Charting the Strategy for Internationalization

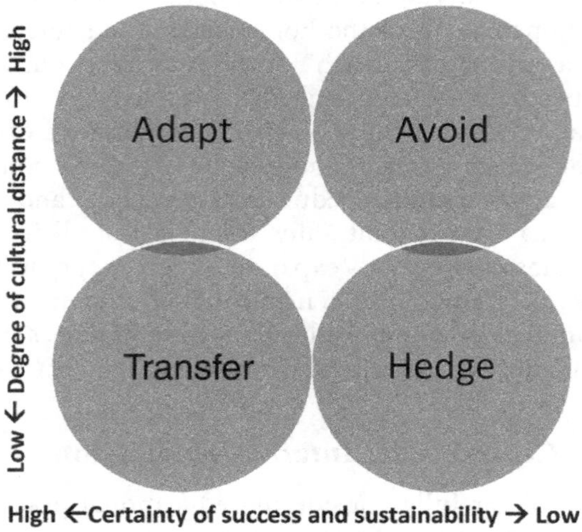

Source: Adapted from Wilkins and Huisman (2012).

Although it is easy to reflect that partnerships involving high cultural distance and low commitment and support are easy to avoid, institutional decision maker's desire for the reputational and monetary benefit of partnerships may cloud their vision of the real risks involved.

It is essential, therefore, to adopt a critical perspective to evaluate the appropriateness of any given cross-border internationalization strategy for student learning and development, resulting in a conclusion to transfer, adapt, hedge, or avoid the practice.

Student Learning and Development

Student learning is widely recognized as a prime objective of higher education. As explained further in Chapter 7, student learning is integrally connected to student development (NASPA & ACPA, 2004). Student learning and developmental outcomes are a documented attribute of high-impact institutions where learning and development are recognized as occurring across the entire university experience; yet the ubiquitous nature of learning is sometimes unrecognized.

Learning Outcomes.   Learning outcomes have long existed in western/northern colleges and universities and have grown in breadth, depth, and complexity. The concept of learning outcomes became the basic building blocks of the Bologna reforms as well (EUA, 2007). From its inception, the Bologna process sought to identify disciplinary-based competencies, later called outcomes, to promote student learning, transferability of credit, and to meet labor needs. This process also identified general competencies across disciplines identified in the *Tuning Bologna* model (Adelman, 2009).

In the United States, the Association of American Colleges & Universities (AAC&U, 2010) has given leadership to a widely adopted, commonly defined set of outcomes. Presented in Liberal Education and America's Promise (LEAP) (http://www.aacu.org/leap/vision.cfm), these essential learning outcomes relate both to disciplinary studies as well as to general outcomes from the university experience. They include: (1) *Knowledge of Human Cultures and the Physical and Natural World* through the study of such fields as language, history, and science; (2) *Intellectual and Practical Skills*, including critical and creative thinking, communication, teamwork, and problem solving practices across the curriculum; (3) *Personal and Social Responsibility*, including civic engagement, ethical reasoning, and intercultural competence (4) *Integrative and Applied Learning*, including applying knowledge and skills to new complex problems.

A strength of US higher education is the role of student life in promoting learning, development, and student success beyond the classroom. The Council for the Advancement of Standards in Higher Education (CAS, 2015), a 35-year-old US and Canadian consortium of 42 professional associations, has established over 40 standards of practice in student affairs and services that address a set of outcomes, including the domains of *knowledge acquisition, construction, integration, and application*; *cognitive complexity*; *intrapersonal development*; *interpersonal competence*; *humanitarianism, and civic engagement*; and *practical competence*. CAS standards have been adapted in numerous regions around the world.

A philosophy of learning and development that can influence the overall environment, the thesis of this volume, is that development of student outcomes is the responsibility of those who provide educational experiences both in the classroom and beyond the classroom. *Learning Reconsidered* (NASPA & ACPA, 2004) stressed the critical nature of "vibrant educational partnerships among members of the academic faculty and student affairs professionals in which all campus educators share broad responsibility for achieving defined student outcomes" (p. 35). Indeed, the recent Gallup/Purdue study (2014) of graduates and employers demonstrated diverse college factors such as mentoring, long-term projects, and participation in student organizations that contributed to workplace engagement and personal well-being.

The use and related assessment of university outcomes is expanding internationally. Recently, the Organisation for Economic Co-operation and Development (OECD) piloted their Assessment of Higher Education Learning Outcomes (AHELO) project with 17 countries or regions. Their study sought to determine the feasibility of assessing common skills in the disciplines of economics and engineering along with a set of generic skills independent of disciplines.

Understanding the Student Experience

As the preceding sections illustrate, how a student engages during college impacts the learning and developmental outcomes they achieve and their overall student success.

Considerations Related to the Classroom.   If broad and deep impact is desired in the classroom, comfortably and naturally infusing an international perspective across a variety of disciplines, courses, and related experiences is a must. Knight's (2012) "at home" and "cross-border" framework demonstrates that faculty and academic administrators have numerous elements that can be included in a comprehensive strategy that will repeat common themes and build on values and learning outcomes that have the potential to permeate an entire institution.

"At home" methods of internationalization include infusing international, cultural, or comparative perspectives in existing courses or creating new courses that do. Modifying teaching and learning processes through virtual experiences, inclusion of international experts, and introduction of research and scholarly work from other cultural settings are other "at home" methods. Research involvement, co- and extracurricular involvement, and liaison with local or regional cultural groups can also offer "at home" opportunities. Most of these share a contextual limitation—they are internationalization within the confines of what is essentially a national or regional perspective. An example of a pervasive internationalization model that originates from a national perspective is evident in Singapore's 21st-century competencies (Singapore Ministry of Education, 2014).

"Cross-border" internationalization, as noted previously, involves moving people, processes, pedagogies, or entities across national or regional lines. Probably the most ambitious internationalization effort of this type is the European Union's Bologna process. Although the largest number of students benefiting from the access and mobility fostered by Bologna and now Erasmus are students with EU passports; the changes brought by these policy statements and changes have also made European universities more attractive to students throughout the world. European Commission (2016) highlighted significant gains for students who studied across national borders in employability characteristics such as tolerance for ambiguity, decisiveness, and vigor.

Opening national borders throughout the EU is seldom referenced as study abroad, but it is much like what happens when United States students utilize study abroad as one of their internationalization experience. Study abroad by United States students is likely to increase as a result of the "Generation Study Abroad" commitment of 150+ universities to doubling the number of United States students who make this a part of their academic experience (http://www.iie.org/Programs/Generation-Study-Abroad). And, the presence of international students studying in the United States, the

NEW DIRECTIONS FOR HIGHER EDUCATION • DOI: 10.1002/he

United Kingdom, Australia, and other countries continues to rise (http://www.iie.org/Research-and-Publications/Open-Doors), although trends and preferences of where to study are often moderated by visa approvals, finance, or home country policy and funding. International students who study in another country are most often perceived as the only ones benefiting from this when, in fact, if domestic students welcomed international students as a resource and actively sought to learn from them, all would benefit. Engaging with international students is not only an untapped resource but sometimes is perceived negatively. For example, recent analysis of Canadian students' views of international students conveyed mixed opinions (Lambert & Usher, 2013), perhaps emblematic of the cultural gap yet to be recognized and bridged as students from all cultural/national backgrounds encounter each other. Successful cultural encounter, and growth toward cultural competence is not well understood and is difficult work, especially because students in the early stages of their own maturational processes are not only uncomfortable with "others" but may have many questions about themselves.

One of the more challenging aspects of adopting or adapting contemporary educational practices from the west relates to active learning pedagogy. Those students who have been socialized in cultures in which deference to authorities, personal humility, and affiliation with the group is the norm, may find active learning to be a particularly difficult stretch.

There are many other possibilities for infusion of international perspectives in cross-border academic partnerships. The most important point is that internationalizing the curriculum will be more successful when it is comprehensive, when it occurs in multiple synergistic experiences, recognizing both the intellectual and personal development journey that learners are encountering.

Considerations Beyond the Classroom.   From access, recruitment, admissions, and retention, to career advising, mental health counseling, residential life, campus activities, leadership and service, sports and recreation, student government, health and well-being, and financial aid advising are all examples of the range of necessary programs and services that stretch beyond the classroom. Altbach (2009) observed that "student development and student affairs are now seen as a key task of most academic systems—and with good reason" (p. xiii). Although Altbach recognizes student affairs work for supporting student success, it is also widely regarded (see *Learning Reconsidered*, NASPA & ACPA, 2004) for its educational and developmental contributions to college outcomes. In that regard, many student affairs staff members may also be seen as educators in the co-curriculum.

Not only has student affairs been recognized as critical to student learning and development in North America, other regions of the world have advocated and are increasingly asserting the importance of enhancing student learning throughout students' experiences (Woodard et al., 2004). As an

NEW DIRECTIONS FOR HIGHER EDUCATION • DOI: 10.1002/he

example, for nearly 20 years, the Asian Pacific Student Affairs and Services Association (APSSA) has offered conferences with themes such as Serving Increasingly Diverse Student Populations (1996) and Promoting Students' All Round Development (2008).

In a 2009 UNESCO publication, Ludeman, Osfield, Hidalgo, Oste, and Wang (2009) documented the state of student affairs and services in numerous countries. This publication was significant in starting the conversation about what student affairs and services had to offer international higher education and provided essential grounding for what is becoming a much more robust conversation. Writing in the same UNESCO publication, Ludeman and Strange (2009) acknowledge that "Student affairs and services professionals are key players in the advancement of the talents of all nations" (p. 6). They identify a set of principles, values, and beliefs that can be used to support and guide student affairs and student services (see Table 1.1) as higher education institutions pursue various internationalization strategies.

Ludeman et al. (2009) stimulated what is now becoming an international movement dedicated to analyzing and refining higher education practice across national borders. Although international convergence has yet to unfold, it is clear that many contributions have been made through western/northern higher education practice.

Considerations Related to Integration.   Ultimately, it is the integration of students' experience both in the classroom and beyond the classroom that may be most important of all; students typically experience these complex settings seamlessly. Some internationalization offerings very naturally integrate in and out of class dimensions. Service learning is an example in which many institutions find that the most effective approach combines student development staff maintaining relationships in the community, encouraging cultural openness, and managing legal and logistical factors while faculty provide disciplinary perspectives, research evidence, and inquiry processes to the mix. Such a shared responsibility in international service learning is a very powerful tool to bridge the intellectual and personal development aspects of students' learning.

Although some North American practice in student affairs has become more professionalized and consequently compartmentalized, the early educators who advocated for improved student support and focus on learning and development viewed this responsibility as one shared among faculty, staff, and students (Roberts, 2012). As educators create new opportunities designed to address the broader challenge of internationalizing their institutions that are proposed in this book, a full partnership among faculty, staff, and students is likely to be required as well (Schuh & Whitt, 1999).

Conclusion

This volume seeks to enhance student learning and development by creating a dialogue about international education practices, allowing for cultural

Table 1.1. Key Principles for Internationalizing Student Affairs and Student Services

Purposes and partnerships	Be consistent with the institutional mission
	Be student centered (acknowledge students as partners and responsible stakeholders)
	Promote lifelong learning
	Promote learning for life
	Use seamless delivery integrated with the academic mission
	Build and nurture robust partnerships among faculty and student affairs educators
Access and diversity	Attract and retain a diverse student body
	Ensure culturally sensitive practices
	Cultivate human capacity for work and community development
	Align access goals with the needs of local, regional, and national vision
Learning and development	Apply critical cultural perspective when adapting practices from others
	Address the personal and developmental needs of students as whole human beings
	Promote independent, self-directed student behavior
	Address three major transitions of moving into university, through university life, and into career and workplace
	Recognize learning is complex and multifaceted
	Prioritize academic and career counseling
	Use information technology to facilitate the student learning process
	Build supportive and inclusive learning communities, locally and globally
Resource management	Adhere to codes of ethics and use of effective management practices
	Ensure diverse funding sources that include significant institutional support
	Fund technology that is central to effective management
Research and assessment	Provide systematic inquiry related to how students' experience can be documented and enhanced
	Use assessment data to improve programs and services

Source: Adapted from Ludeman and Strange (2009, pp. 5–9).

adaptation, that draws together the work of policy makers, faculty, management, and student affairs and services staff. This volume focuses on the broad experiences of university student learning and development achieved through intentional practices in the curriculum and co-curriculum. We present ideas that we hope are equally compelling for faculty and staff members in higher education, whether they work in class, out of class, or in the infrastructure support systems that allow excellence in learning and development to thrive.

References

Adelman, C. (2009). *The Bologna process for U.S. eyes: Re-learning higher education in the age of convergence*. Washington, DC: Institute for Higher Education Policy. Retrieved from www.ihep.org/Research/GlobalPerformance.cfm

Altbach, P. G. (2009). Introduction. In R. Ludeman, K. Osfield, E. Hidalgo, J. Oste, & H. Wang (Eds.), *Student affairs and services in higher education* (pp. xiii–xix). Paris, France: UNESCO.

American Council on Education, Center for Internationalization and Global Engagement. (2014). *About CIGE*. Retrieved from http://www.acenet.edu/news-room/Pages/Center-for-Internationalization-and-Global-Engagement.aspx

Association of American Colleges and Universities. (2010). Liberal education and America's promise. Retrieved from http://www.aacu.org/leap

Council for the Advancement of Standards in Higher Education. (2015). *CAS professional standards for higher education* (9th ed.). Washington, DC: Author.

Duderstadt, J., Taggart, J. & Weber, L. (2008). The globalization of higher education. In L. Weber, & J. Duderstadt (Eds.), *The globalization of higher education* (pp. 273–290). London, UK: London Economica.

European Commission. (2016). *The ERASMUS Impact Study Regional Analysis*. Retrieved from http://ec.europa.eu/education/library/study/2016/erasmus-impact_en.pdf

Gallup/Purdue University. (2014). *Great jobs, great lives*. The 2014 Gallup-Purdue Index Report. Retrieved from http://www.gallup.com/strategicconsulting/168791/gallup-purdue-index-inaugural-national-report.aspx

International Association of Universities. (2012). *Statement on globalization: Affirming academic values in internationalization of higher education—A call for action*. Retrieved from http://www.insidehighered.com/blogs/globalhighered/affirming-academic-values-internationalization-higher-education-call-action#ixzz1sZVUaMJC

EUA. (2007). *Bologna—An overview of the main elements: Qualification frameworks*. http://www.eua.be/eua-work-and-policy-area/building-the-european-higher-education-area/bologna-basics/Bologna-an-overview-of-the-main-elements.aspx

Knight, J. (2004). Internationalization remodeled: Definitions, rationales, and approaches. *Journal for Studies in International Education, 8*, 5–31.

Knight, J. (2012). Concepts, rationales, and interpretative frameworks in the internationalization of higher education. In D. Deardoff, H. De Wit, J. Heyl, & T. Adams (Eds.), *The SAGE handbook of international higher education* (pp. 27–42). Thousand Oaks, CA: Sage.

Kuh, G. D. (2008). *High-impact educational practices: What they are, who has access to them, and why they matter*. Washington, DC: Association of American Colleges and Universities.

Kuh, G. D., Kinzie, J., Schuh, J. H., Whitt, E. J., & Associates. (2005). *Student success in college: Creating conditions that matter*. San Francisco, CA: Jossey-Bass.

Lambert, J. & Usher, A. (2013). *Internationalization and the domestic student experience*. Toronto, Canada: Higher Education Strategy Associates. Retrieved from http://higheredstrategy.com/wp-content/uploads/2013/10/Intelligencebrief7-HESA-internationalization-FINAL-WEB.pdf

Ludeman, R., Osfield, K., Hidalgo, E., Oste, J., and Wang, H. (Eds.). (2009). *Student affairs and services in higher education*. Paris, France: UNESCO.

Ludeman, R. & Strange, C. (2009). Basic principles, values and beliefs that support an effective student affairs and services programme in higher education. In R. Ludeman, K. Osfield, E. Hidalgo, J. Oste, & H. Wang, (Eds.), *Student affairs and services in higher education* (pp. 5–9). Paris, France: UNESCO.

National Association of Student Personnel Administrators and American College Personnel Association. (2004). *Learning reconsidered: A campus-wide focus on the student experience*. Washington, DC: Authors.

Oketch, M, McCowan, T, & Schendel, R. (2014). *The impact of tertiary education on development: A rigorous literature review*. London: Institute of Education. Retrieved from http://r4d.dfid.gov.uk/pdf/outputs/HumanDev_Evidence/Tertiary-education-2014-Oketch.pdf

Pascarella, E., & Terenzini, P. (2005). *How college affects students* (Vol. 2). San Francisco, CA: Jossey-Bass.

Roberts, D. (2012). The student personnel point of view as a catalyst for dialogue: 75 years and beyond. *Journal of College Student Development, 53*, 2–17.

Roberts, D. (2015). Internationalizing higher education and student affairs. *About Campus, 20*(2), 8–15.

Schuh, J. H., & Whitt, E. J. (Eds.). (1999). *Successful partnerships between academic and student affairs*. New Directions for Student Services, 87. San Francisco, CA: Jossey-Bass.

Singapore Ministry of Education. (2014). *21st century competencies*. Retrieved from http://www.moe.gov.sg/education/21cc/

Stiglitz, J. E. (2013). *The price of inequality: How today's divided society endangers our future*. New York, NY: W.W. Norton.

Tight, M. (2014). Working in separate silos? What citation patterns reveal about higher education research internationally. *Higher Education, 68*, 379–395.

Wilkins, S. & Huisman, J. (2012). The international branch campus as transnational strategy in higher education. *Higher Education, 64*, 627–645.

Woodard, D. B., McClellan, G. S., Resendiz, J., Marques, C., Ouanhua, Z., Kwandayi, H., ... Wilcock, P. (2004). *The global practice of student affairs/services: An international survey*. University of Arizona, Center for the Study of Higher Education.

DENNIS C. ROBERTS *was associate provost of Hamad bin Khalifa University and assistant vice president for education with the Qatar Foundation from 2007–2014. He is past president of the American College Personnel Association (ACPA) and has authored 4 books and over 50 book chapters and other articles on student affairs, student learning, and leadership.*

SUSAN R. KOMIVES *is professor emerita in the Student Affairs Program at the University of Maryland. She is past president of the Council for the Advancement of Standards in Higher Education, ACPA, and editor of the* Handbook for Student Services *along with other books and articles on student leadership.*

2

This chapter examines the underlying motivations behind why institutions and organizations decide to apply particular policies and practices. By applying a lens of five diffusion models— learning, imitation, competition, normative, and coercion—to understand these motivations, decision makers and implementers will make better choices for internationalization based on their specific context.

Student Learning in an International Context: Examining Motivations for Education Transfer

Darbi Roberts

What types of programs, services, and opportunities do educators offer students in a new and internationalized higher education context? How do they decide what programs and services to borrow from whom, and why do they decide to borrow them? This chapter builds on the groundwork presented in Chapter 1 by determining how institutions and practitioners decide what kinds of international education "best practices" to implement in an international context. As Roberts and Komives outlined (based on Wilkins & Huisman, 2012), there are four choices institutions make when applying best practices across borders and contexts. Institutions *transfer* best practices when cultural distance between institutions is low and commitment and support for the initiative is high. When cultural distance is great but commitment and support is still high, programmatic *adaptation* occurs by fitting the initiative into the new context. An institution decides to *hedge* in using an initiative if the cultural distance is low but commitment is low as well. And finally, institutions may *avoid* an initiative or partnership if the cultural distance is high and the commitment to making it work is low. The purpose of this chapter is to understand how universities and practitioners go about deciding what practices for internationalization to borrow, either consciously or subconsciously, and why they decide to use those practices.

In their foundational work, DiMaggio and Powell (1983) posit that when an area of practice becomes established, homogenization ensues. In

NEW DIRECTIONS FOR HIGHER EDUCATION, no. 175, Fall 2016 © 2016 Wiley Periodicals, Inc.
Published online in Wiley Online Library (wileyonlinelibrary.com) • DOI: 10.1002/he.20195

other words, when many people perform similar tasks such that a profession or area of study emerges, the people doing that work tend to replicate or mimic the practice as the field grows. "Early adopters" do so out of a desire to innovate and improve performance. As the innovation becomes widespread and is adopted more widely, the innovation is no longer seen as progressive but rather something one does to gain legitimacy or maintain status quo. The innovation becomes normative. This process is also referred to by DiMaggio and Powell as "isomorphism," meaning that programs and institutions will come to resemble others that face a similar set of conditions within their environment. This chapter explores this process, because there are many ways in which others influence programs and institutions. DiMaggio and Powell laid out several predictors of isomorphic change, including:

- Institutions that depend on other institutions are more likely to become more similar to those institutions on which they depend.
- The more uncertain an institution is about its future and how to get there, the more likely it will "model itself after organizations it perceives to be successful" (p. 154).
- Ambiguous goals lead to modeling after others are deemed successful.
- The more managers in an institution participate in professional associations, the more likely their organization will become like other institutions in the same field.
- The smaller the number of institutional models, the faster same-ness will grow.
- Same-ness increases with professionalization of a field.

Building on this idea of isomorphism, Berry and Berry (2014) explain why an institution might decide to adopt an innovation or model after others. They give two explanations, the first of which is based on internal determinants, or characteristics of an institution that influence its decision to make change. Internal determinants are explored throughout this volume by examining specific contexts of each country, higher education system, or institution. At this point, it is simply important to keep in mind that certain internal determinants of universities and higher education systems will influence the likelihood of the adoption of an innovation, including but not limited to: organizational size, levels of resources, number and strength of the obstacles to innovation, availability of resources to overcome those obstacles, motivation to innovate, presence of individual advocates for specific ideas or innovations, coordinated groups to champion an issue, timing of the innovation, and the extent to which the institution has previously adopted or was open to innovation (Berry & Berry, 2014). The presence or absence of all of these things within an institution or higher education system could influence their likelihood of adopting a new innovation.

Table 2.1. Stakeholders in Higher Education

	Government Sector	Education Sector	Private Sector
Systems	Ministry of education Federal government State/provincial government Multinational organizations (such as UN or EU)	National higher education systems National higher education governing bodies	Different industries, such as technology, manufacturing, services, arts and culture, entrepreneurial, finance
Institutions	Governmental agencies	Universities (varying types) World Education Services, Institute of International Education, and other nonprofit educational service organizations Professional associations Accreditation and quality assurance boards	Any business that hires graduates Alternative for-profit educational providers (such as KAPLAN, ETS, or College Board in the United States) Think tanks and independent research organizations
Individuals	Policy makers Lobbyists	Students Parents Faculty Administrators	Business owners Hiring managers Investors

Another determinant that is particularly important in higher education is the age of the institution or system (Berry & Berry, 2014). New institutions or systems approach innovation and change very differently from well-established ones. In many ways, the absence of institutional history may allow for greater experimentation but with greater risks for failure for the sheer fact that they have no reputation upon which to build (or to be kept afloat if it fails).

Stakeholders

In addition to considering how and why new ideas spread, it is important to identify the stakeholders in the process. Table 2.1 gives a glimpse into the myriad of players in the higher education industry who impact or are impacted by the spread of ideas around internationalization. One can view this on many levels from the macro (systems on the country level) to the micro (individuals within each system themselves), and also by sector (government, education, and private). To better understand why and how ideas

New Directions for Higher Education • DOI: 10.1002/he

spread, examples from varying levels will be used to illustrate the concepts. Each sector will look structurally different in various countries and some countries may have more sectors than these three. A helpful task for the reader is to highlight and add stakeholders they identify in their own countries. Taken on an institutional level, the same exercise could help identify which key players are part of the internationalization movement within their own university.

Diffusion Models

So, how do educational systems and institutions decide what aspects of internationalization to borrow from whom, and why do they decide to borrow them? In the policy literature, Berry and Berry (2014) identify five different "diffusion models" that explain why policies, programs, and ideas are diffused and adopted. In science, diffusion is defined as the movement of molecules from an area of high concentration to low concentration. So, too, in higher education, diffusion of ideas entails the movement of programs, policies, and practices from entities who use them to those who do not. Thus, the diffusion models discussed here are the methods by which internationalization programs, policies, and practices move across the higher education industry, both within a country and throughout the world.

Isomorphism is a direct outcome of diffusion, and, in the context of internationalizing higher education policy, diffusion is a primary means of creating isomorphism. Understanding diffusion models, therefore, is key to understanding isomorphism because we cannot understand why things are becoming the same if we do not understand why institutions are choosing to adopt each other's practices. Stakeholders and innovation readiness play a role in diffusion, and, therefore, in isomorphism, by shaping how a new policy or program is diffused. As Berry and Berry (2014) describe it: "diffusion occurs if the probability of adoption of a policy by one [entity] is influenced by the policy choices of other [entities] in the system" (p. 310). In other words, diffusion happens when an institution or system chooses to implement a new program, policy, or practice because another institution or system implemented it first. There are a number of scenarios for how this plays out, and the rest of this chapter is devoted to those particular scenarios or what we will refer to as "diffusion models" going forward.

Learning.   The first diffusion model Berry and Berry (2014) discuss is *learning*, which "occurs when policymakers in one jurisdiction derive information about the effectiveness (or success) of a policy from previously adopting governments" (p. 310). As a result, an innovation has a high probability of being borrowed by one entity because the innovation is perceived to be effective in the context in which it had previously been implemented. The likelihood of diffusion increases as the environmental similarities between the borrowing institution and the reference institution increase. For example, a liberal arts college in the United States may choose to increase

NEW DIRECTIONS FOR HIGHER EDUCATION • DOI: 10.1002/he

the number of language programs it has to offer as a part of the effort to "internationalize" the curriculum, thus preparing and encouraging students to study abroad. Over five years, the college doubled the number of foreign languages it teaches, particularly in nonromance languages like Chinese and Swahili, and as a result the number of students traveling to Chinese- and Swahili-speaking countries dramatically increased. Meanwhile, another liberal arts college in the United States also wants to internationalize their curriculum, and perceives that the first college was very successful in internationalizing by offering more foreign language classes, and, therefore, decides to do the same to try to achieve the same outcome.

Imitation.   The second diffusion model is *imitation* or *mimetic*, which occurs when one entity perceives another entity as "worthy of emulation," compelling the imitating institution to adopt any innovation the imitated institution possesses, regardless of the effectiveness of the innovation itself (Berry & Berry, 2014, p. 311). DiMaggio and Powell (1983) characterize the mimetic process as happening primarily in cases of uncertainty, when "goals are ambiguous," environments are new or indiscernible, when problems have undefined causes and/or indistinct solutions (p. 151). Imitation is then a way to deal with uncertainty in a way that disassociates the imitator from the success or failure of the borrowed solution. The reference institution serves as a convenient model or source of ideas. Imitation happens unintentionally and indirectly as a result of faculty or staff turnover and cross-pollination. It can also happen explicitly as a result of the influence of consulting organizations that may implement the same solution on multiple campuses. The avoidance of imitation may explain why developing institutions in former colonies resist any semblance of transferring or adopting practices from higher education in their colonial past.

Imitation is particularly likely among peer institutions. For instance, "University of X" has a number of institutions it calls its "peers" or "aspirational peers" such that they typically look to those other institutions for ideas of how to tackle certain problems. University of X is trying to increase its international student enrollment and so it surveys what its peer institutions are doing to tackle this issue. Finding that its peers are increasing international student enrollment, University X adopts this strategy regardless of the fact that it may involve many different complexities, drivers, and goals. The Office of Admissions at University of X may not have a full picture of all of these drivers and goals, but it knows that most of its peer institutions are drastically increasing international recruitment efforts in China through frequent recruitment trips to all the top universities in that country, and therefore does the same. University of X does not exactly know how effective its peer institutions are in their recruitment trips, but decides to plan them anyway because they want to keep up with what their peer institutions are doing.

Normative.   Berry and Berry's (2014) third diffusion model is that of the *normative process*, which happens primarily through the process of professionalization. A primary activity of professional associations is to define and promulgate a set of normative rules, standards, and/or best practices for organization structure and professional conduct. Not only do these normative rules create similarity in duties and roles across the profession (i.e., international education) itself, these normative rules also produce a pool of professionals who take on similar positions at a range of institutions and often move between similar jobs in other institutions, implementing similar practices across institutional type, regardless of the fit of those practices with the institution's cultural context. On an institutional level, the normative influence of professional associations can take on a "bandwagon effect" as well, whereby the borrowing institution decides to adopt an innovation "not because it is imitating any particular university or learning from the experience of other adopters, but rather because it observes that the innovation is being widely adopted by other universities, and because of shared norms" (p. 312).

Consider the way in which professional organizations, such as the European Association of International Education, the International Association of Universities, and other European-based professional associations, create and disseminate standard statements of good practice in internationalization of higher education. Other organizations across the world do this as well, but because of the unique pressures of the Bologna Process in Europe and the fact that the majority of European countries aspire to conform to the norms of the European Higher Education Area (EHEA), countries in this region are particularly likely to conform to standards and rules set out by well-respected professional associations in the region. This is particularly evident in the conformity of the 3–2 degree across Europe (3 years in bachelors, 2 years in masters). Previously, each country had its own structure for the bachelors, masters, and doctoral degrees. Because of the increased pressure for student mobility and transferability of degrees, countries throughout Europe began to conform to the 3–2 model. As more countries adopted this new model, more countries felt compelled or pressured to conform, even though there was no specific policy mandating that they adopt this model. The EHEA is a particularly interesting case because there is no governing body that imposes its authority on the countries or institutions within the boundaries of the EHEA. However, because of the mechanisms of normative diffusion, most if not all countries have conformed to a similar model for their degree structures. The Council on the Advancement of Standards in Higher Education (CAS) plays a similar role in the United States by disseminating a broad array of standards in various functional areas within institutions regarding the student experience. What is particularly interesting about the CAS standards is that, although the organization explicitly states that the standards are developed for United States context, institutions all over the world still use them to influence policy and practice. As a result, CAS standards have a very different sort of normative effect by becoming the initial framework adapted for local purposes.

Competition.   The fourth diffusion model is *competition*, which is primarily driven by the desire to gain an advantage over something or someone else. Innovations diffuse as a result of competition when the decision to adopt a new idea is "motivated by the desire ... to achieve an economic advantage over other jurisdictions or, equivalently, to prevent other jurisdictions from securing an advantage over it" (Berry & Berry, 2014, p. 312). For higher education, competition could be driven by the fight for a number of different resources, including rankings (and the prestige they entail), funding, students, and top faculty, particularly in scenarios in which those resources are scarce, in which staunch rivalries between entities exist, or in which there is a threat of new competitors or substitutes for the product (i.e., education) being offered.

Competition can be a driver among institutions within the same higher education system, among institutions in different higher education systems, and also between higher education systems from different countries. All institutions compete, but particularly those at the elite level vie for the best students, the highest rankings, the most funding, and the best faculty, on both a national and international scale. As attention to global rankings increases and as international student and faculty mobility increase, so too does competition among universities worldwide. Many countries across Europe and Asia, as well as Canada and Australia, are beginning to create national strategies for the internationalization of higher education that explicitly identify methods and strategies for improving the quality of their higher education systems and institutions. These methods often involve improving metrics such as recruitment of international students and the number of students that study outside the country, as well as improving global rankings, all with the primary goal of raising the comparative and competitive status of that country's higher education system. They adopt new national policies from other countries to gain the advantage, as well as to keep other countries from gaining an advantage over them. For example, Country A wants to attract more international students to its institutions than Country B, but Country B has looser visa policies toward students. Therefore, Country A adopts either the same or more relaxed visa policies as Country B to gain a competitive advantage by making it easier for students to study there, thus increasing the flow of students to Country A over Country B.

Coercion.   The fifth and final diffusion model, *coercion*, is perhaps the most difficult to grasp in terms of the mechanism of diffusion itself. Coercion can result from both formal and informal pressure, and among institutions that share a common environment or common and/or shared challenges (DiMaggio & Powell, 1983). Institution A is coerced into adopting an innovation when "a more powerful [institution] B takes action that increases A's incentive or, in the extreme case, forces A to adopt" (Berry & Berry, 2014, p. 313). Power dynamics are key in this model, as coercion is more likely to happen in cases where one institution has greater power over another. An example of this type of direct power-driven coercion can be seen often in international institutional partnerships. The more power-ful and prestigious institution may have strict admissions standards that the weaker institution may be either directly forced into using as a part of the partnership agreement or strongly incentivized, through restriction of funding or other means, to implement as a result of the mere association with the more prestigious institution. Coercion can also be seen as a collective process when "one or more [institutions] take actions that create an incentive for another [institution] to adopt a policy" (Berry & Berry, 2014, p. 313). Collective coercion often happens when a group of institutions take action together through agreements among conferences or other academic coalitions. For example, if a few of the United States Ivy League institutions decided together to adopt a policy that allowed doctoral students to unionize, then the other Ivy League institutions would follow suit. Similarly, if the Ivy League as a whole decided to allow doctoral students to unionize, it is likely that many other elite institutions in the United States and abroad would also enact such a policy. This diffusion model is best characterized by the phrase "as Harvard goes, so goes the country." Replace "Harvard" with Oxford, Cambridge, Peking, or Tsinghua, or replace "country" with "world" and a similar dynamic emerges.

Applications to Internationalization

These five diffusion models—learning, imitation, normative, competition, and coercion—help us begin to understand why and how ideas about internationalization spread throughout the worldwide higher education industry. There is a significant amount of overlap between them, and institutions often exhibit more than one type of diffusion model for any given innovation adoption. Institutions and governments make decisions about adopting new policies for a variety of reasons, and these diffusion models are intended to help make sense of these reasons. Table 2.2 helps differentiate each diffusion model by their main drivers and common conditions under which they occur.

Being conscious of the motivations that encourage institutions to consider practices of another is critical because exposing the motivations may actually help decision makers make better choices. For examples in which imitation may be underway, raising questions about whether the practice makes sense for the borrowing institution can then be raised more easily. Or when competition is the driving force, institutions are then encouraged to critically examine if the practice will actually pay off to a degree that justifies the cost in time and resources.

Conclusion

Shared practices and standards of professionalism are often a good thing for ensuring commonality of student experience and quality of the work of

Table 2.2. Differentiating Diffusion Models

Type	Main Driver	Common Conditions
Learning	Effectiveness of the policy being transferred or adopted	Low cultural distance between entities
Imitation	Worthiness of an institution to be imitated (policy is irrelevant)	Ambiguous or uncertain goals, environment, problems, and solutions Poorly understood organizational technologies
Normative	Ubiquity of the adoption Desire of institution to conform	Low cultural difference between entities Presence of shared values and norms
Competition	Desire to gain an advantage	Resource scarcity Threat by new or alternative providers and products Territorial dispute
Coercion	Adoption is incentivized (both positive and negative)	Differential in power between two institutions Collective action

international education. Nonetheless, the diversity in institutional and cultural settings within a country and between countries demands that practitioners carefully consider their motivations and intentions for borrowing innovations and ideas in international education from other contexts. Because of significant imbalances in global power dynamics among countries and institutions, many of the diffusion models have the potential to mask neocolonialism. Although "best practices" promote quality and comprehensiveness, they also can serve normative and/or coercive hidden agendas to shape industry in a particular desired fashion. The goals of this chapter have been to bring some of those motivations to light to aid in this critical consideration and to help inform future decision making.

References

Berry, F. S., & Berry, W. D. (2014). Innovation and diffusion models in policy research. In P. A. Sabatier & C. M. Weible (Eds.), *Theories of the policy process* (3rd ed., pp. 307–362). Boulder, CO: Westview Press.

DiMaggio, P. J., & Powell, W. W. (1983). The iron cage revisited: Institutional isomorphism and collective rationality in organizational fields. *American Sociological Review*, 48, 147–160.

Wilkins, S., & Huisman, J. (2012) The international branch campus as transnational strategy in higher education. *Higher Education*, 64, 627–645.

DARBI ROBERTS is an assistant dean of student affairs at Columbia University's School of International and Public Affairs, with an EdD in International Education Development from Teachers College. She worked in Doha, Qatar, for an American university in student affairs for several years and works with a predominantly international student population at Columbia.

NEW DIRECTIONS FOR HIGHER EDUCATION • DOI: 10.1002/he

3

Predicated on the principles of success and contextuality, this chapter shares an African perspective on a first-year adjustment programme, known as First-Year Village, including its potential and challenges in establishing it.

First-Year Village: Experimenting With an African Model for First-Year Adjustment and Support in South Africa

McGlory Speckman

My aim in this chapter is to share best practice on first-year adjustment from an African context. By African I do not necessarily mean the entire continent as a unit but I propose South Africa as a specific region that may represent dynamics occurring elsewhere. This delineation is made due to the disparate practices of the various regions of Africa that are divided along the lines of Francophone, Anglophone, Portuguese, and German—associations with their former colonial origins as determined by the Berlin Conference 1884–1885. The potential of these to forge a more organised and internationally attuned body is only now beginning to emerge with some countries being affiliated to American student affairs associations (Schreiber, 2014).

In addition to locating myself in the southern tip of Africa, I also declare at the outset, that owing to job change and staff movement, sustained monitoring and nurturing of the project initiated at the University of Zululand in 2013 and piloted in 2014 presented in this chapter proved to be a challenge. Therefore, the input of this chapter is more of a perspective than a sharing of best practice.

The chapter is predicated on two basic principles, namely, that: (1) the goal of all student support is student success and (2) in order for it to be effective, student support has to be contextual. First-year adjustment does not happen in a vacuum but with the view to inculcating good practice and healthy habits that are essential for students' success throughout their careers as students. The proposed model creates conducive conditions for this to happen.

NEW DIRECTIONS FOR HIGHER EDUCATION, no. 175, Fall 2016 © 2016 Wiley Periodicals, Inc.
Published online in Wiley Online Library (wileyonlinelibrary.com) • DOI: 10.1002/he.20196

Context and Purpose

The primary purpose of the model, known as First-Year Village (FYV), is to provide support and nurture to first-year students in a communal environment as they adjust to a post-school context. It is a designated physical space where first-year students live together in university residences with peer mentors under the joint supervision of student affairs and faculty staff. A secondary purpose is to ensure the safety of first-year students while they are dealing with their newfound freedom and vulnerability, which might otherwise expose them to opportunists or distract them from their academic goals and ambitions.

Professional counsellors advise that contrary to a common assumption of self-sufficiency, most first-years need this kind of support. Research on attrition at the University of Pretoria where both the top-end and average student were interviewed confirms this (Lemmens et al., 2008). So did a mentorship programme which was launched by this author at the beginning of the same year. Indeed, most South African students come from backgrounds of economic, social, and political deprivation and are in need of material support, social integration, and orientation on issues of democracy and justice (Waghid, 2010) after being made to feel, through various social institutions, that they are the "insignificant others" (Levinas, 1987). These come to bear when they are on their own in an environment that can be intimidating. Peer mentors are especially valuable for social adjustment and psycho-social support.

Adapting Models and Frameworks

Although the FYV model emanated from the strategy of a specific institution to improve its student support and throughput rate, it is not out of sync with international student support theories (Speckman & Mkhize, 2014). For example, the model incorporates aspects of the theory of "integrated student support" which draws attention to a continuity between "in-class" and "out-of-class" learning, thereby calling for a greater cooperation between "faculty" and "college" (Keeling, 2004). The aim is not only to develop cognitive skills but also to inculcate values of responsible citizenship (Hamrick, Evans & Schuh, 2002). For this reason, emotional and material needs are also considered important. Tinto (2008) who invested time in working with students from disadvantaged backgrounds observes that "access without support is no opportunity" (p. 3). Support in this context also included understanding the socio-economic backgrounds of students, their material needs and appropriate interventions (Tinto, 2008).

Two things have to be clarified about the proposed model. First, it is not a replacement of the existing student support models, ranging from psycho-social to academic development, but an enhancement thereof. Secondly, while not discounting a student's social capital, the model recognises the need for a transfer of wisdom from the experienced to what those in the United States refer to as "freshman" or first-year student. It is therefore an enabling mechanism for these things to take place.

In South Africa, "village" refers to more than just a small settlement that does not qualify to be a town. The term connotes traditional communal living which is sustained by value systems and kinship solidarities (Masango, 2005) or in Durkheim's 1997 language, "mechanical and organic relationships." Individuals are thus part of a chain of relationships and they each constitute a special link in this chain. The village assumes a collective responsibility for the success of an individual or individuals (Masango, 2005) and this obligation supersedes the temptation for competition. Thus, individuals are affirmed and their potential nurtured.

It is in a village where, as a result of the aforementioned ties, people share the little or plenty they possess, where solidarities are formed, not only on the basis of biological kinships but around a social cause or causes because of people's awareness that they need each other (Masango, 2005). In fact, African scholars understand this to be *"Ubuntu"* and "caregiving" (Masango, 2005; 2006) which incidentally makes one's place of origin or ethnic affiliation irrelevant. Allegiance is paid to whoever is in authority. This provides an excellent model of support particularly for first-year students whose vulnerability may delay their adjustment and affect their performance. Experience of more than a decade shows that association, whether religious, political, academic, or of a personal nature, do not only help individuals to adjust but they also create a sense of belonging, that is, a sense of community. Some lifelong relationships begin during this difficult period.

There may be a thin line between the FYV and the Living-Learning Communities as established by some of the affiliates of the Association of College and University Housing Officers International (ACUHO-I). However, they should not be confused. Living-Learning Communities as advertised in the brochures of Pennsylvania and Central Arkansas, for example, seem to be predicated on the philosophy of learning beyond the classroom which finds expression in a context of *like-minded people* (my emphasis). Hence thematic topics and learning communities are advocated. Georgetown offers a wide-range of these, including academic support. Its variations, for example, the Listen, Living-Learning Communities (LLLC) of South Africa's Stellenbosch University are also undergirded by the former philosophy and they work with themes. The philosophy of a FYV on the other hand, may be summed up in the following manner: "with others around me, everything is possible." In other words, "a person is a person through persons" (Villa-Vicencio, 1996). This is empowering to those who have had several hurdles to conquer, in order to reach the university level.

The appropriateness of the approach in a context where deficiencies are transferred from primary level (known as basic education in South Africa) is questionable. There are constant academic exchanges among students in open spaces although there are no measurable outcomes. These are complemented by formal debates and other extramural activities. Resources must instead be devoted to academic support, emotional support, and material support. Values and principles involved in helping each other as well as methods applied, contribute to an individual's development. Interestingly, Tinto notes in a different context that students do form support groups on their own (Tinto, n.d.). This is the communal spirit encouraged in a FYV.

Descriptions of Program

Available spaces in the village are limited to the percentage of first-year accommodation provided by the institution in a given academic year. At the University of Zululand, about 30% of available accommodations were reserved for first-year students in 2014. Selection was based on academic merit, financial clearance, and need. Applicants were advised upfront about the village and its aim. They elected to be part of the village. Some of those who lived outside campus expressed disappointment at not being included. Hence the ruling that they could participate in activities if they identified with the objectives of the village. It would, however, be disingenuous to describe admission as voluntary in a situation where accommodations were in demand.

Unlike the themes or topics around which Living-Learning Communities are organised, students in the village live according to faculties, that is, those studying commerce, live together; those in natural sciences live together, etc. Mentors are chosen according to the academic disciplines background. Embracing diversity begins in the faculty context, then it moves to the village context. Owing to limited space in this chapter, I will only list the features of the village as they appear in the *Shape and Size* document of UNIZULU (Speckman & Mkhize, 2014) without getting into the contents.

Mentors, who provide accompaniment for the first-years as they find themselves on their own in a complex environment. Matching is not with mentors but solidarity groups. This may take up the entire first semester and is known as "extended orientation."

- *Adjustment programmes*, which are aimed at assisting the individual to adapt both socially and academically, involving cultural and spiritual activities.
- *Goal setting*, which is part of accompaniment and assists the individual to set academic and personal goals.
- *Time management skills*, whose aim is to assist students to reap maximum benefits from their time at the institution.
- *Cognitive skills*, such as research and writing, study skills.
- Outcomes based *cocurricular and extramural activities*, which are campus-based during the second semester.

NEW DIRECTIONS FOR HIGHER EDUCATION • DOI: 10.1002/he

It might be argued that most of the features mentioned normally constitute a mentorship module. This is true save that instead of individuals, mentors in the FYV are expected to work with groups or "communities," divided according to academic disciplines and subfields. They are available for individual support if necessary but they work mostly with referrals to professional staff.

Resources Required for Success. The project needed human and financial resources. As part of the planning, two of the unfilled posts of wardens, otherwise known as house parents or house coordinators, were earmarked for the postgraduate students who would serve as the extension of the house parents and faculty staff in the village. Duties included assisting with academic matters, ensuring discipline, supervising peer mentors, facilitating house gatherings, and role modelling. Instead of cash remuneration, peer mentors received accommodation and meals.

Peer mentors are senior undergraduate students who are performing well academically, have had an experience of the university, are resourceful with answers pertaining to daily life, and have leadership skills. They are selected through a careful process and are trained in the areas in which they are expected to perform as mentors. The recommended number of mentees per mentor is 12 or less.

Management, faculties, and university council were lobbied at separate fora and the project received support. Owing to the involvement of the University Council, financial support was guaranteed, especially because the council endorsed the strategy of inculcating skills, values and habits that should help students at the time of their study and later, as citizens.

Challenges, Future Directions, and Recommendations. A major challenge associated with the process of establishing a separate village for first-years was opposition from student leadership based more on a perceived loss of student political power than a rejection of the philosophy. This results from a culture of student formations (i.e., affiliations) playing chief hosts to first-year students, which has developed over the years. The bone of contention arises because FYV limits access to first-year students by undesignated groups. At one university, student leaders claimed not to be against the concept but the processes that led to the establishment of the village, whereas at another, the project was indefinitely abandoned. In the first instance, extensive, recorded consultation had taken place. Hence the students had no case.

Regarding resources, the institution should finance the village if it is accepted as one of the drivers of institutional goals. Costs involved are calibrated to the budget of an ordinary residence budget. Assistant house parents are appointed against an existing post or two. Mentors need not be full-time staff but could also be senior students who act as role models. On the one hand, this brings the mentor closer to the world and experiences of first-year students, but, on the other hand, it saves the financial resources of the institution.

NEW DIRECTIONS FOR HIGHER EDUCATION • DOI: 10.1002/he

My recommendations include the following:

- Consultations with faculties for support of the concept, as well as the after-hours tuition.
- Consultations with the student leadership so that they do not see the village as a fragmentation of the student body but as an advantage for the first-years.
- Advertising of the peer mentor positions, interviews, and training at least three months before the arrival of first-year students.
- Decide what attributes the village is intended to inculcate and include them in the training of mentors.
- More student affairs professionals have to be lobbied to support and promote the concept.
- Mechanisms must be built in to measure impact as part of project enhancement.
- Documentation of the project as it develops.

References

Berlin West Africa Conference (1884–1885). General Act of the Berlin Conference.

Durkheim, E. (1997). *The division of labour in society* (Trans. I. Hall) New York, NY: The Free Press.

Hamrick, F., Evans, N., & Schuh, J. (2002). *Foundations of student affairs practice: How philosophy theory and research strengthen educational outcomes.* San Francisco, CA: Jossey-Bass.

Keeling, R. P. (Ed.). (2004). *Learning reconsidered: A campus-wide focus on the student experience.* Washington, DC: NASPA/ACPA.

Lemmens, J., Du Plessis, G. I., Rai, L. C. J., De Klerk, M., Mitchell, Y., Julie, V. J., ... van Niekerk, J. H. (2008). *Exit interviews at the University of Pretoria-full report.* Education Innovation. Unpublished report.

Masango, M. (2005). The African concept of caring. *HTS, 61*(3), 915–925.

Masango, M. (2006). African spirituality that shapes the concept of Ubuntu. *Verbum Et Ecclesia, 27*(3), 930–943.

Levinas, E. (1987). *Time and the other* (Trans. R. Cohen). Duquesne University. Retrieved from www.monoskop.org/File Levinas Emmanuel_Time_and_The_Other _1987.Pdf

Schreiber, B. (2014). Key challenges facing student affairs: An international perspective. In M. Speckman, & M. Mandew (Eds.), *Perspectives on student affairs in South Africa* (pp. 9–26). Somerset West, South Africa: African Minds.

Speckman, M., & Mkhize, Z. (2014). *The shape and size of student affairs and services at UNIZULU.* Unpublished plan presented to Council of UNIZULU June 30, 2014.

Tinto, V. (2008). *Access without support is not opportunity.* Keynote address. National Institute for Staff and Organisational Developmen, University of Texas.

Tinto, V. (n.d.) *Taking student retention seriously.* Retrieved June 24, 2012 from www.marin.edu/word-PPT/Taking Retention Seriously.pdf

Villa-Vicencio, D. (1996). *Spirit of freedom: South African leaders on religion and politics.* Berkeley: University of California Press.

Waghid, Y. (2010). Re-imagining higher education in South Africa: On critical democratic education. *South African Journal of Higher Education, 24,* 491–494.

McGLORY SPECKMAN is currently a professor in the New Testament Studies Department at the University of Pretoria. He is a former dean of students at the same university and a former executive member of the South African Association of Senior Student Affairs Professionals (SAASSAP) where he served for two terms as research and development officer.

NEW DIRECTIONS FOR HIGHER EDUCATION • DOI: 10.1002/he

4

Helping students who were born under China's 1979 One Child Policy learn to face adversity was the target of multiple programs during first- and second-year study. Carefully planned and embraced by academic colleagues, students receive academic credit for "whole person education."

Adversity Training for Chinese University Students

H. C. J. Wong

China has recently abolished its One Child Policy initiated in 1979 by Deng Xiaoping. Under this policy, social benefits for having multiple children are given up in order to limit population growth. Consequently, cohorts of university students, the "90s generation," come almost entirely from "single child families." This chapter describes how one private university in China chose to promote resilience in response to the unique characteristics of these students using the UNESCO five pillars of learning (the 5 Learnings) as a framework:

- Learning to know,
- Learning to do,
- Learning to live together,
- Learning to be, and
- Learning to transform oneself and society for a sustainable future. (UNESCO, 2005)

Context and Purpose: Chinese Students in Transition

Some educators believe that single children suffer from weaker social skills. Astonishingly, the contrary is true. Generally, Chinese students are very outgoing and sociable. Realizing the need to develop social skills, parents compensated by sending their kids early to kindergarten. Social deficits are made up through early interactions with peers in such settings as piano classes and talent centers (Feng, 1993).

However, difficulties arise when it comes to intimate relationships. For example, university roommate relationships are a big problem because Chinese young people do not compromise in matters related to living. Since

NEW DIRECTIONS FOR HIGHER EDUCATION, no. 175, Fall 2016 © 2016 Wiley Periodicals, Inc.
Published online in Wiley Online Library (wileyonlinelibrary.com) • DOI: 10.1002/he.20197

they are seldom if ever rejected by their parents, it is hard for them to accept that things may not turn out the way they think. Therefore, it is not uncommon that some students will try to bend the rules, "rightfully" (Wang & Liu, 1983).

Intimate relations, of course, include romantic love. The lack of compromising skills does not help them to develop mature and loving relationships (Zhao, 2011). On one extreme, some relationships break up due to conflict and, on the other extreme, they devolve into submissive dissatisfaction. On another level, knowledge about sexual diseases does not encourage safe sex behavior among university students (Pan, 2011). Safe sex practices are not adopted simply because students are incapable of saying "no" to their partners.

Another problem among the 90s generation is their narrow definition of success, predominantly understood in terms of career income and prestige. This explains why they waste months staying home instead of going to work as general laborers, because engaging in low-status work causes them to lose face. Most students come from families of upper middle income; they are fortunate as compared to their fathers who have gone through economic hard times and deprivation. In short, they are less ready for hardship. Although overgeneralization should be avoided, these trends are quite prevalent (Feng, 2013).

How, then, can universities help students face adversities in public and personal life? As more and more Chinese students go overseas to study, student affairs professionals elsewhere want to know more about their characteristics. Particularly when Chinese students do not mix well with local and other international students, concerns are raised. Effective adversity management programs to prepare these Chinese students arouse interest in China as well as perhaps being of interest to other countries.

Adapting Models and Frameworks: Changing Concepts of Resilience

The ability to cope with adversity, or to bounce back after personal failure or community disaster, is resilience. Resilience is not an inborn ability but a coping skill to be learned and a protective network to be developed. As pioneers, Steve Wolin and Sybil Wolin (1993) developed their concepts of "Resilient Self." They identified seven resiliencies: (1) insight, (2) independence, (3) relationship, (4) initiatives, (5) creativity, (6) humor, and (7) morality.

Almost at the same period, Wagnild and Young (1993) developed their Resilience Scale. They suggested that resilience is a set of five characteristics: (1) meaningful life (purpose), (2) perseverance, (3) self-reliance, (4) equanimity, and (5) existential aloneness, or coming back to one self. The 25 items compose 2 subscales: a 17-item "Personal Competence" subscale and an 8-item "Acceptance of Self and Life" subscale (Wagnild, 2009).

Subsequently, Scales and Leffert (1999) developed a 40-item Developmental Assets Scale, which was later widely used in assessing effectiveness of youth programs. The 40 assets can be divided into two dimensions: internal and external. Under internal assets there are the three factors of (1) support, (2) empowerment, and (3) constructive use of time. For external assets, the four major factors are (1) commitment to learning, (2) positive values, (3) social competencies, and (4) positive identity.

Description of Program

A more recent conceptualization suggested three ways of how resilience works. They can be called the three models of resilience: compensatory, protective, and challenge models. Assets are defined as characteristics residing within the individual such as competence, coping skills, and self-efficacy. Factors external to the individual, such as parental support, adult mentoring, or community organizations, are defined as resources (Fergus & Zimmerman, 2005). The three models describing the interplay of individual assets and external resources were very useful to guide our resilience education program design at the Beijing Normal University Hong Kong Baptist University United International College, Zhuhai, China.

Enhancing Student Resilience Resources and Assets. New students begin with a focus on learning to live together. Other universities in China arrange dormitories by gender, by year, by department, and by divisions. We allow students to choose roommates of different years and different majors to mix in the same residence blocks. Gender is not mixed because of parents' concern. Without siblings, when life crises emerge after their parents pass away, from whom can our students seek help? Coworkers or schoolmates will be their major sources of support. Mixing students of different academic majors and different years helps to broaden their social networks.

Based on the same concept of social support network, a Mentor Caring Program (MCP) divides all Year 1 students in small groups of 15 to 20. One faculty member of the same academic discipline is assigned to serve as their mentor, assisted normally by two peer mentors who are in their senior years. MCP groups hold casual and fun events at least once per semester, whereas Mentors will meet with their mentees individually also once per semester.

As soon as freshmen arrive, a series of University Life Education (ULE) workshops are embedded in the orientation calendar. ULE begins before formal teaching and focuses on independent self-management, or "learning to be" oneself. ULE allows students to have a full semester to work on a project in which they will be asked to read a book, interview a person, and write an essay. Daily life topics are included in these modules while direct real-life experiences of interacting with strangers are purposefully part of the process. Module topics of ULE include: (a) socialization and

Table 4.1. WPE Experiential Learning Program (Study Plan)

Year	Section	Modules	Units	Remark
Year 1	I	Experiential Development Program (EDP)	1	Required
	II	Emotional Intelligence Camp (EI Camp)	1	Required
Year 2	III	Sports Culture	1	Select either one
		Experiential Arts	1	
	IV	Voluntary Service	1	Select either one
		Environmental Awareness	1	
Special	–	Adversity Management Camp *(AM Camp)	1	Optional
Minimum Requirement: Four Units				

*Restricted to students who have fulfilled the minimum four-unit requirement.

communication, (b) love and sex, (c) career planning, (d) leadership, (e) money management, (f) stress management, (g) law and crime, (h) time management, (i) self-awareness, and (j) goal setting.

ULE, MCP, and the New Students' Self-Discipline Squad Training (SDST) together form the year-one experience. Conventional military training, required by the government, is modified to emphasize self-discipline. Students attend a full day workshop before they take part in four days of physical training. Precedent cases of violations of university regulations are presented to students to let them know that delayed gratification and self-control are keys to future success in life (Mischel, 1966). SDST is certainly echoing ULE, because self-discipline is an important component of "learning to be."

To facilitate "learning to do," students are encouraged to form academic societies, interest clubs, and service groups. Student Affairs Office (SAO) staff facilitate but do not determine student group activities as long as they are law abiding and consistent with university regulations. SAO provides leadership training, which is structured into three tiers for beginners, organizers, and leaders. Servant leadership is emphasized in an international perspective. A Leadership Path Scheme enables students to accumulate points from attending all kinds of faculty or student activities. At the end, they will receive a portfolio for extracurricular engagement in university life, indicating the level of leadership award (i.e., Bronze, Silver, Gold, or Diamond Servant Leadership Award) that they have attained through accumulation of activity points.

To achieve the UNESCO five learnings and break the barriers between extracurricular and curricular learning, the university adopted a "curriculum approach" to organize "Whole Person Education" (WPE), experiential learning by nature. WPE accounts for only four out of the total 132–136 credits but are required for graduation eligibility. Table 4.1 presents the structure of the WPE study plan.

NEW DIRECTIONS FOR HIGHER EDUCATION • DOI: 10.1002/he

The Experiential Development Program challenges students to complete difficult tasks in a team. It uses adventure experiences to test and cultivate mutual trust, self-motivation, team cooperation, and positive attitude. Many graduates cite EDP as one of their most memorable learning experiences at the university.

Emotional Intelligence Camp reflects what typically happened in the workplace. Students are required to form a business proposal while being videotaped. They design a product, think about its marketing strategy, develop its promotion media, and compete for the best business plan award. Their performance in each round of competition determines the kind of food they get for lunch and dinner. On one evening, they work overnight to meet deadlines, which is not unusual in real work life. Physical fatigue is the most difficult enemy for emotional control. Breakdowns or inability to control emotions, videotaped, will lead to deduction of marks in the business-proposal competition. In the process, students learn to control their emotions and do not let emotions control them.

In China, university students are encouraged to participate in voluntary services, in accordance with the socialist doctrine. However, service learning, with clear educational outcomes, defined knowledge base, and skill sets, is relatively new to educators in China. The learning process involves both information-giving sessions, as well as community service participation. Students are required to submit journals and reflective writings for evaluation purposes. If they opt for attending an Environmental Awareness Module, the structure of the learning processes is similar, with the only difference being that their community service will be related to ecological issues.

Adversity Management Camp is by design the most challenging. A few years back, students were taken to an island to carry out adventurous activities just like other Jungles or Outward Bound camps. To enhance the transference of adjustment skills learned from outdoor hardship to handle situations in real life, recently a simulation activity called "City Challenge" was added. Students are given very limited pocket money and they have to earn their food by selling products they invent. They experience personally that poverty, leading to hunger, thirst, shame, and anger, is one of the most extreme forms of adversity.

Resources Required for Success.   Numerous factors made the experiences in the program successful. Direction from top university leaders is a precondition, and support from academic departments is also essential. In 2015, at least 125 faculty members, including lecturers and assistant professors, served as Mentors for the Mentors Caring Program. Faculty members are also appointed to coordinate the Whole Person Education Modules, notably from the academic Programs of Applied Psychology, Social Work, and Social Administration and Environmental Science. For University Life Education, professional counselors are deployed to conduct self-management

NEW DIRECTIONS FOR HIGHER EDUCATION • DOI: 10.1002/he

workshops. For Self-Discipline Squad Training, official military officers are invited to conduct physical training.

Quality assurance is rigorous. Being credit bearing, Whole Person Education courses are accredited according to procedures exactly the same as for other academic courses. Students are required to submit journals, reflective writings, and essays that will be scrutinized by external examiners.

Adhering to evidence-based decision making is always emphasized. A number of tests are used in the process to measure effectiveness. Among them are the Six Seconds' Social Emotional Index, Seligman's Values in Action Scales, and Wagnild's Resilience Scale.

Financial and human resources required for all these Student Affairs and Whole Person Programs are substantial and indispensable. Incorporating such expenditures into tuition guarantees their implementation.

Challenges and Future Directions: Are We Successful?

Feedback exercises for University Life Education are utilized to determine the success of these programs, whereas formal teaching evaluations are conducted for the Whole Person Education courses. Included in the Graduate Survey is a section on Character Strengths (Park, Peterson, & Seligman, 2006) to check whether students have acquired positive values and thinking skills. However, further comprehensive and scientific studies on program impacts are needed to demonstrate how successful we are in transforming these One-Child-generation students into resilient individuals. Time-series studies to follow up on our students in the first decade after graduation are even more desirable to monitor resilience.

All in all, broadening student social networks will enhance their future resilience resources, cultivating self-management skills will equip them with resilience assets, and exposing them to simulated challenges, hopefully, will develop their compensating resilience. As reported in *Graduates Surveys*, most students found themselves changed significantly during their days in university. Whole-person development broadly defined in both the curricular and extracurricular arenas are among their most striking memories of university life.

References

Feng, X. T. (1993). Prejudice and reality, education problems for single child survey and analysis, *Sociological Studies, 1*, 93–99.

Feng, X. T. (2013). *Study on problems of single child in China*. Beijing, China: Economic Science.

Fergus, S. & Zimmerman, M. A. (2005). Adolescent resilience: A framework for understanding healthy development in the face of risk. *Annual Review of Public Health, 26*, 131–132.

Mischel, W. (1966). Theory and research on the antecedents of self-imposed delay of reward. In B. A. Maher (Ed.), *Progress in experimental personality research* (pp. 85–131). New York: NY: Academic Press.

Pan, H. L. (2011). *Sex knowledge and safe sex among university students.* Final Year Project, Social Work and Social Administration Program, Beijing Normal University Hong Kong Baptist University United International University.

Park, N., Peterson, C. & Seligman, M. (2006). Character strengths in fifty-four nations and the fifty US states. *The Journal of Positive Psychology, 1*(3), 118–129. Retrieved from http://dx.doi.org/10.1080/17439760600619567

Scales, P. & Leffert, N. (1999). *Developmental assets: A synthesis of the scientific research on adolescent development.* Minneapolis, MN: Search Institute.

UNESCO (2005). *United Nations decade of education for sustainable development (2005–2014): International Implementation Scheme.* Retrieved from http://unesdoc.unesco.org/images/0014/001486/148654e.pdf

Wagnild, G. M. (2009). A review of Resilience Scale. *Journal of Nursing Measurement, 17*(2), 105–113. doi:10.1891/1061-3749.17.2.105

Wagnild G. M. & Young H. M. (1993). Development and psychometric evaluation of the Resilience Scale. *Journal of Nursing Measurement, 1*(2), 165–178.

Wang, Y. F. & Liu, R. Q. (1983). Re-examing the problems of single child: A study on school performances of single child, *South China Population, 4*, 49–52.

Wolin, S. J. & Wolin, S. (1993). *The resilient self: How survivors of troubled families rise above adversity.* New York, NY: Villard Books.

Zhao, X. (2011). Psychological problems of single child and its remedies. *Sci-Tech Magazine, 30*, 12–13.

H. C. J. WONG *is chief of student affairs and professor in social work and social administration, Beijing Normal University Hong Kong Baptist University United International College, Zhuhai, China. His research interests include disaster social work, healthcare social work, youth work, psychosocial resilience, service learning and community engagement for higher education.*

5

This chapter describes a programme of learning and development at the University of Sheffield, United Kingdom, to support looked-after children and care leavers (youth previously provided care outside or beyond family) throughout the student lifecycle. In this context, looked-after children are those cared for by a town/city authority where parent(s) are not able to provide suitable care.

Who Cares for Care Leavers?

Julie Askew, Paul Rodgers, Andrew West

Higher education in the United Kingdom (UK) originated with the medieval establishment of the universities of Oxford and Cambridge. Those institutions established from the 19th century onwards were largely created by "royal charter" and there is a historical pattern of central government funding alongside local management with considerable autonomy allowed to individual universities. In the 1960s, a second sector of higher education was recognised in the form of "polytechnics" and the distinction between institutions was later abolished in the 1990s (Skinner, 2006). There are now around 2.5 million students studying at more than 160 higher education institutions in the UK.

Context and Purpose

The most recent substantive government policy statement on Higher Education (Department for Business, Innovation, and Skills, 2011) draws attention to the historical partnership between state funding and institutional autonomy, and places an increased emphasis on accountability to students. Mirroring trends in other higher education systems, changes in student financial arrangements has seen a rebalancing away from direct government grant to institutions towards funding via individual student loans. The political debate speaks of universities coming under competitive pressure to provide better quality at lower cost. In a more diverse higher-education sector, government is emphasising the student learning experience, with a growing focus on improved information for prospective students, student charters, and more transparent tracking of graduate outcomes, levels of employment, and salary as part of a narrative around the "value" of higher education.

NEW DIRECTIONS FOR HIGHER EDUCATION, no. 175, Fall 2016 © 2016 Wiley Periodicals, Inc.
Published online in Wiley Online Library (wileyonlinelibrary.com) • DOI: 10.1002/he.20198

Adapting Models and Frameworks

Developing alongside this is an emphasis on the "student experience," a term increasingly used to encompass the totality of a student's life within higher education—not only in the classroom but also incorporating cocurricular activities and support. This development is in line with the trends mentioned in the first chapter in this volume whereby the academic mission of universities is seen to be carried out by a variety of programmes, both inside and outside the classroom. This broad view of education is reflected in recent research concerning student perceptions of the whole higher education experience (Ali & McLaran, 2012). At the same time, student services professionals have re-framed their contribution no longer in terms of a "safety net" for students with problems but rather as pro-active provision for all students in support of academic success. Increasingly services teams provide support to other institutional staff, including faculty, who need assistance in student issues.

Student Services now typically cover areas such as widening participation into higher education (including support for groups like the care leavers discussed in this chapter), progression and retention, financial literacy, international student support, well-being services, student induction and transition, academic development, employability, citizenship promotion, safety and risk management. In view of this breadth of contribution, there is an increasing trend for student services to be given a level of priority alongside activities such as teaching and research in terms of institutional strategic planning and in resource allocation (AMOSSHE, 2009, 2010; Universities UK, 2002). These developments can be seen to closely reflect points made in the introductory chapter of this volume, that is, that student affairs is now seen as a key task (Altbach, 2009) and student services professionals key players in the global educational endeavour (Ludeman & Strange, 2009).

The University of Sheffield Setting

The University of Sheffield has expanded from an original intake of around a hundred students in 1905 to a current student community of 26,000 within a large research-intensive institution spanning a broad range of subject areas. The University's foundation aim was to bring higher education within reach of the children of the people working in the large industries of Sheffield. The institution now welcomes a hugely diverse range of staff and students from more than 130 countries, offering a quality educational experience enhanced by a research-led environment (Mathers, 2005).

The Student Services Department at the University of Sheffield has a broad remit incorporating the whole student lifecycle from recruitment, through registrar, to educational strategy and faculty support. There is also a range of student support services, alongside activities supporting career development. Student Services encompasses around 600 staff, and a common strategic framework binds the work of the whole team, explicitly reflecting institutional values and objectives. Student services are characterised by collaboration, and the various teams foster strong links with departments throughout the university. Over recent years, the university has invested significantly in its student-facing services, including a new health centre, a huge redevelopment of residential accommodation, and a rebuild of the students' union complex (West, 2010).

Description of Program

The university's support for looked-after children and care leavers exemplifies its approach to partnership and collaboration throughout the student lifecycle. Definitions of a looked-after child can vary. In UK legislation, a looked-after child is one for whom a local authority has obligations to provide care of a child or young person under 16 where parent(s) or guardians(s), for whatever reason, are prevented from providing suitable care. Three quarters of the approaching 70,000 looked-after children in England are placed in short- or long-term foster care with smaller numbers placed in residential homes or kinship care with extended family, or in secure settings (HM Government, 2015a). More flexible definitions are commonly used in the higher-education sector to make support available to anyone who is "care experienced."

The university became more aware of the importance of supporting young people from care around 2006, when the children's charity BUTTLE UK (BUTTLE UK, 2015) introduced its national Quality Mark. This provided a framework for higher education institutions to define, improve, and accredit their support for looked-after children and care leavers to help them aspire to higher education and to support them throughout their studies. It recognised excellence in the policy and practice of universities, and those that acquired the Mark were expected to provide the following support as a minimum:

- A named contact to give specific support and advice before, during and after application to university.
- Additional specific financial support.
- 365 days accommodation throughout undergraduate study.
- Help and support with transition to higher education.

The University of Sheffield acquired the Quality Mark in 2007, setting out its intentions to provide support throughout the student lifecycle, and galvanising teams—particularly within Student Services—to support matters such as pre-entry outreach; recruitment and application; transition into higher education; retention; and successful academic attainment.

The Quality Mark acted as a catalyst across the UK to help change practice within higher education, with significant numbers of institutions taking part, and approaching 200 gaining accreditation during the life of the scheme. Although the Mark is now no longer awarded, BUTTLE UK still provide information for stakeholders to support the recent establishment of the government-backed Statement of Commitment to Looked-After Children and Care-Leavers in Education (HM Government 2014a).

Meanwhile the need for increased multiagency support for care leavers became more evident in 2007 following the UK government publication *Care Matters: Time for Change* (Department for Education and Skills, 2007), building on the previous *Care Matters: Transforming the Lives of Children and Young People in Care* (HM Government, 2006). Both papers identified barriers to the educational progression of looked-after children emphasising the need for partnership work. These publications promoted the following improvements:

- Better identification of care leavers who apply to university, via a formal declaration within the national applicant system.
- A bursary scheme, requiring town/city authorities to provide a one-off payment of £2000 to care leavers who progress to university.
- Encouragement of universities to offer better-targeted outreach work, staff training, and further support to young people in care.

Reflecting these policy drivers, designated staff within Student Services at the University of Sheffield now identify and contact care-leaver applicants at the earliest opportunity to provide a named contact and offer support; in some cases, this may allow for adjusted academic entry criteria following receipt of evidence of previous disrupted studies. The introduction of the applicant declaration has enabled this process, although in practice some applicants are unsure of their status, or might not declare due to concern about labelling; meanwhile agencies are working together to reassure and inform applicants that it is helpful to declare as early as possible to benefit from the best support (The University of Sheffield, 2015). Excellent national resources exist to provide reassurance and comprehensive information and guidance to those from care, and to their advisers (NNECL, 2015; Propel, 2015; UCAS, 2015).

The university's outreach team provides pre-entry activities for children and teenagers to raise their aspirations towards higher education; to support high school attainment; to help familiarisation with the university environment, and to build confidence. Such activities for care leavers have generally been adapted from preexisting work aimed at other disadvantaged learners.

The university's programme of support has evolved significantly since 2007, involving renewal of Quality Mark accreditation in 2010 and 2013, when the university achieved "exemplary" status, in recognition of its effective practice. A newly established pool of "Looked-After Children's Champions"—current student role models who were former care leavers—has been highly beneficial in conveying the message "If I can do this so can you." The following student reflection exemplifies the value "being a LAC Champion has given me the opportunity to make a difference by being a positive role model and enthusing children about learning. I have gained hugely from the role as it has allowed me to develop transferrable skills which will increase my employability."

Relationships have been forged with town/city authorities and other universities in the region to benefit ongoing developments. Networks of stakeholders and practitioners across the UK, and into Europe, have also been established to share best practice. Current activities are summarised in Table 5.1.

Resources Required for Success.   Collaboration across the student lifecycle has enabled the university to embed care-leaver support in the broader range of service provision. Rather than new roles being created, support has typically been developed within existing teams. A resources overview is in Table 5.2.

Although a relatively modest non-staff budget (approximately $16,000 USD annually) is allocated to this work across the teams indicated, a far larger sum goes to students as financial support. In 2014, approaching $300,000 was provided in care-leaver scholarships and a further $21,000 in targeted hardship payments, to around 30 students in total.

Challenges and Future Directions

In spite of the many support initiatives mentioned earlier, only around 6% of English care leavers enter higher education at the age of 19, compared to 48% of a similar age in the general population. High school attainment presents a similarly differential picture, with only 12% of those in care achieving the generally accepted educational benchmark, compared to 52% of those not in care in 2014. When set alongside statistics demonstrating a 15% growth in the care population in England over the period from 2007–2014, it is clear that work to support young people in care is growing in importance (HM Government 2014b, 2015b).

The university's approach continues to develop. Future initiatives include developing additional guidance for faculty admissions tutors across the university; and establishing an internship for a care-leaver graduate. Building on a firm basis, we remain committed to supporting the needs of this important group of students, throughout their learning journey and beyond.

NEW DIRECTIONS FOR HIGHER EDUCATION • DOI: 10.1002/he

Table 5.1. The Student Journey

Pre-Entry Outreach	Admissions	Finance	Student Support	Learning and Teaching	Careers
Access to designated contacts in Student Support before and during university study					
"LAC Champs" care leaver students as role models, giving the message "If I can you can"	Guidance calls to applicants who are care leavers from trained LAC Champs	Enhanced financial support via scholarships and tuition fee reduction	365 day housing guarantee throughout the course of study		Skills tracker, CV and interview workshops, internships and placements available to all students
"Go Further Go Higher" University tasters & summer schools for young people in/from care	Consideration of previous disrupted studies during application process	Local authority financial support for care leavers in HE	Student mentors for all students	Study/skills support classes and workshops available to all students	
Transition to HE events and information for care leavers		Postgraduate scholarships available for disadvantaged students including care leavers	Tailored support including help with accessing financial assistance and liaison with external agencies		Trained LAC Champs develop transferable skills and experience
Homework club for younger looked after children					

University contribution to national initiatives (eg "Care Leavers Week") via social media and events

An annual conference and development events for teachers, local authority staff and careers
Development of tailored guidance publications and web-pages
Sharing of best practice through local, national and international networks
Partnership working with local colleges and universities

Table 5.2. Proportion of Role Assigned to This Program

Staff Team	Human Resources (% of full-time role)
Outreach	Activities Officer 40%
	Clerical Officer 25%
	Outreach Manager 5%
Admissions	Admissions Officer 10%
Finance	Financial Support Officers 7%
	Financial Support Manager 2%
Support	Support Officers 12%
	Support Manager 5%

References

Ali, U., & McLaran, A. (2012). *Student experience research: Part 1—Teaching & Part 4— First year student experience.* London, UK: National Union of Students. Retrieved from http://www.nus.org.uk/en/news/research-publications

Altbach, P. G. (2009). Introduction. In R. Ludeman, K. Osfield, E. Hidalgo, J. Oste, & H. Wang (Eds), *Student affairs and services in higher education* (pp. xiii–xix). Paris, France: UNESCO.

AMOSSHE. (2009). *Supplement to the Higher Education Funding Council Financial Sustainability Strategy Group report: The sustainability of learning and teaching in english higher education.* London, UK: Association of Managers of Student Services in Higher Education.

AMOSSHE. (2010). *Understanding and measuring the value and impact of services in higher education that support students: A literature review.* London, UK: Association of Managers of Student Services in Higher Education.

BUTTLE UK. (2015). *For children and young people.* Retrieved from http://www.buttleuk.org

Department for Business,Innovation and Skills.(2011). Higher education: Students at the heart of the system. London, UK: Retrieved from https://www.gov.uk/government /uploads/system/uploads/attachment_data/file/31384/11-944-higher-education-stude nts-at-heart-of-system.pdf

Department for Education and Skills. (2007). *Care matters: Time for change.* Retrieved from https://www.gov.uk/government/publications/care-matters-time-for-change

HM Government. (2006). *Care matters: Transforming the lives of children and young people in care.* Retrieved from https://www.gov.uk/government/publications/care-matters-transforming-the-lives-of-children-and-young-people-in-care

HM Government. (2014a). *Care leaver strategy: One year on progress update.* Retrieved from https://www.gov.uk/government/publications/care-leaver-strategy

HM Government. (2014b). *Outcomes for children looked after by local authorities.* Retrieved from https://www.gov.uk/government/statistics/outcomes-for-children-looked -after-by-local-authorities

HM Government. (2015a). *Children looked after in England including adoption: 2014 to 2015.* Retrieved from https://www.gov.uk/government/statistics/children-looked -after-in-england-including-adoption-2014-to-2015

HM Government. (2015b). *Destinations of key stage 4 and key stage 5 pupils: 2012 to 2013.* Retrieved from https://www.gov.uk/government/statistics/destinations-of-key-stage-4-and-key-stage-5-pupils-2012-to-2013

Ludeman, R., & Strange, C. (2009). Basic principles, values and beliefs that support an effective student affairs and services programme in higher education. In R. Ludeman,

NEW DIRECTIONS FOR HIGHER EDUCATION • DOI: 10.1002/he

K. Osfield, E. Hidalgo, J. Oste, & H. Wang (Eds.), *Student affairs and services in higher education* (pp. 5–9). Paris, France: UNESCO.

Mathers, H. (2005). *Steel city scholars: The centenary history of the University of Sheffield.* London, UK: James and James.

NNECL. (2015). *National network for the education of care leavers.* Retrieved from http://www.nnecl.org

Propel. (2015). *Is higher education for me?* Retrieved from http://www.propel.org.uk

Skinner, M. (2006). *The educational system of the United Kingdom.* Washington, DC: American Association of Collegiate Registrars and Admissions Officers.

The University of Sheffield. (2015). *Your student journey: Students from care.* Retrieved from http://www.shef.ac.uk/ssid/student/care

UCAS (2015). *Advice for care leavers.* Retrieved from: http://www.ucas.com/how-it-all -works/explore-your-options/individual-needs/advice-care-leavers

Universities UK. (2002). *Student services: Effective approaches to retaining students in higher education.* London, UK: Universities UK.

West, A. (2010). *JISC InfoNET strategy pilots: Report from the University of Sheffield Student Services Department.* Retrieved from http://www.jiscinfonet.ac.uk/projects /strategy-pilots/

JULIE ASKEW is outreach and widening participation manager at the University of Sheffield.

PAUL RODGERS is the head of student transitions and support at the University of Sheffield.

ANDREW WEST is university secretary at the University of Sheffield.

NEW DIRECTIONS FOR HIGHER EDUCATION • DOI: 10.1002/he

6

Mexico faces numerous social, economic, and political challenges. Higher education institutions provide opportunity for change by educating socially responsible leaders to become civically engaged citizens.

Educating Transformational Leaders in Mexico at Universidad de Monterrey

Alicia Cantón

Mexico's treasures include natural resources, landscapes and coasts, a rich culture, ingenious people, and an enviable geopolitical location. Its economy is ranked second in Latin America and 15 of 194 globally (World Bank, 2015). If managed properly the resources and the economic potential of the country could reflect in quality life and wealth for the 125 million Mexicans, yet 52.3% of the population lives in poverty. In Mexico, 10% of the richest people concentrate 64% of the country's wealth (Esquivel, 2015) and it is among the countries with a higher level of inequality in the world (Solt, 2014). These factors contribute to huge disparities that represent a risk for social stability.

Context and Purpose: Mexico Needs Leaders

Other key challenges for Mexico's development are education, corruption, and insecurity. The OECD (2007) revealed the deficient quality of the education when Mexico scored below the 500 points average in math (406), reading (410), and science (413) in the Programme for International Student Assessment (PISA) test. Despite a 94% adult literacy rate, only 18% of Mexicans between 25 and 64 have completed tertiary education and over 22% of young adults are neither employed nor studying (OECD, 2014). In 2014, Mexico's score (35) in the corruption perception index (CPI) was the worst among the countries of the OECD. In the CPI, Mexico is ranked 103 of 175 when compared to Denmark (92) or the United States (74). The Global Corruption Barometer revealed that 87% of Mexicans think that public officers are corrupt, along with members of political parties (91%), the legislature (83%) and the judicial system (80%) (Transparency International, 2013, 2014). The culture of bribe and corruption extends to other

NEW DIRECTIONS FOR HIGHER EDUCATION, no. 175, Fall 2016 © 2016 Wiley Periodicals, Inc.
Published online in Wiley Online Library (wileyonlinelibrary.com) • DOI: 10.1002/he.20199

sectors of society in Mexico. A study of KPMG revealed that 44% of business companies bribed public servants in order to obtain benefits including speeding up processes and permits (Hayes, Galvan, & Del Castillo, 2008).

Adapting Models and Frameworks: Leadership and Citizenship Education to Strengthen the Democracy

Mexico's economic and social situation is not different from other Latin American countries. The economic, political, and social challenges of the region remain the most unequal of the planet with a Gini coefficient of 0.52 (United Nations Development Programme, 2010). What needs to change in Mexico and in other Latin American countries? The report *La Democracia en America Latina* (Programa de las Naciones Unidas para el Desarrollo, 2004) described poverty, inequality, and democracy as three forces in a triangle that countries need to balance on the road to growth and development. After studying these political systems, O'Donnell (1997) states the need to strengthen the existing democracies and transition into governments with stronger institutions. In a democratic society, the collective goals are based in the common needs and the greater good; the community defines the priorities and the needs. This implies participation of the different sectors of society to discuss and deliberate on the priorities, how to address the problems and what agreements, policies and programs are needed to reach the common goals and interests. Democracies should have accountability and transparency controls preventing government officers and institutions from allocating resources on different purposes.

A strong democracy demands citizens to vote and to raise their voices but also to actively engage in their community. To consolidate the system, it is necessary for citizens to participate in creating the solutions collaborating with all the actors who can implement them including the government, the private sector, and the not-for-profit organizations sector. Through collaboration and engagement, citizens can hold public officers accountable for their government's actions and contribute to preserve the needs of the majority of the population. Is this kind of civic engagement actually happening? In Mexico, results for 2014 of the national survey of political culture reveal that 54% of the population was dissatisfied with the democracy and 78% recognize that society needs to organize and engage with the public and the private sectors to solve the problems yet only 14% actually reported participating in groups or associations (Secretaría de Gobernación, 2012). In Mexico, like in other Latin American countries, one of the challenges to provoke change is to raise political culture and civic engagement.

Educating the civic mind, developing agency, and leadership to enhance democracy should be a priority in order to improve the social and economic conditions. Universities play a critical role to influence society with their intellectual, human, and social capital power, especially if they systematically and intentionally educate their students to become engaged citizens. Higher education is a resource to improve the country's economic competitiveness and to educate the future leaders who can intervene in the public and private sectors pushing to strengthen the democratic system and to bring change. Research shows that Mexican universities can foster civic engagement through curriculum based activities, student life programming and meaningful community service experiences (Cantón, 2011).

Description of Program: Leadership Development at Universidad de Monterrey

The Universidad de Monterrey (UDEM) is a private, not-for-profit institution that embraces the challenge of educating transformational leaders in congruency with its mission to develop students holistically through a personalized model, in an intercultural environment of academic excellence to find transcendence in the service of others. Since its foundation, the humanistic and Catholic inspired essence of UDEM outlines service as the path for plenitude and a resource to contribute to a sustainable society. The student's holistic formation is promoted through systematic and intentional resources that provide multiple leadership development opportunities and to develop the student's social responsibility and social conscience.

The educational model of UDEM relies on active pedagogies connecting the student to current problems within the local community both through academic course work and through cocurricular courses and activities. Besides promoting problem solving through course work and a purposeful community service experience, every student is required to complete an internship at a local organization or public office to design and implement a project and complete an academic capstone project that shows the application of professional competences in response to community needs.

The Leadership Model.   The formative component of the educational model of UDEM is based on a leadership model designed in 2003 and rooted in the concept of transforming leadership as the result of a relational process (Burns, 1978; Komives, Lucas, & McMahon, 1998; Yukl, 1994; See figure 6.1). Based on the leadership definitions of Bennis, McGregor, and others, UDEM began by describing transformational leadership as the human capacity to identify, promote and enact changes in the environment by developing and optimizing the individual capacities in benefit of society. The leadership model was inspired in the four pillars of education of UNESCO (2016): learning to know, learning to do, learning to be, and learning to live together. It works with students' motivations, personality, talents, and skills at the *individual* level, it promotes their interaction with others in the *social* level, and encourages them to find plenitude and realization in life by serving other's needs within their community for the *transcendental* level.

NEW DIRECTIONS FOR HIGHER EDUCATION • DOI: 10.1002/he

Figure 6.1. UDEM's Leadership Development Model

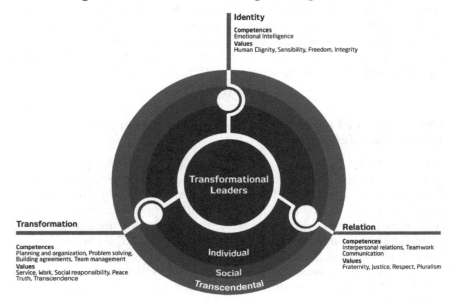

Requirements.   To articulate the leadership model, UDEM uses a component of cocurricular courses that every undergraduate student must complete before graduation to systematically and intentionally develop leadership competences and values. Students choose over 80 cocurricular options in the areas of arts, culture, sports, health, sustainability, social justice, as well as civic and political leadership.

Experiential education is the pedagogical resource for students to build knowledge and skills through active learning (Builes Jaramillo, 2003; Luckner & Nadler, 1997). The four blocks of the UDEM leadership model are shown in Figure 6.2. By actively engaging students in performing arts, in sports training and play, in debate and argumentation as part of a student organization, in missionary work, in fundraising and communication campaigns, and in other activities, students enact their leadership learning. Through this participation, students learn about their strengths, limitations, and capacities and about the need to effectively work with others both in the university and outside, helping them to discover purpose through service while contributing to the needs of the community.

In addition to the cocurricular courses, the conceptual model is rooted in a social formation workshop that precedes students' community service experience thus enhancing their social conscience. Every undergraduate student in Mexico is required to perform 480 hours of service. At UDEM, the service component is carefully managed by seeking to place students in work with impoverished social groups. The service experience seeks to

Figure 6.2. The UDEM Leadership Model

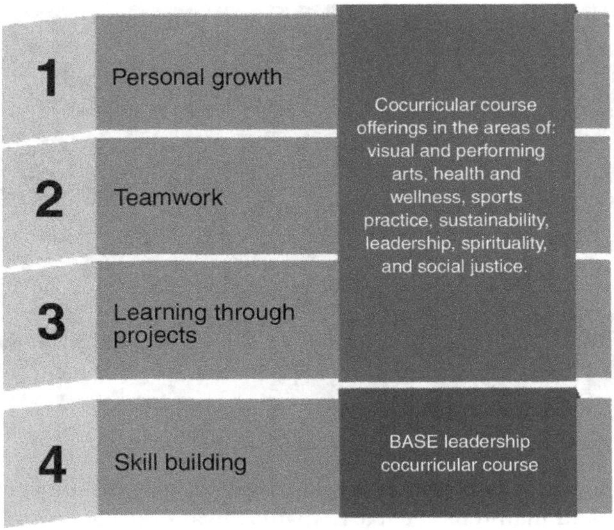

enhance students' social responsibility and awareness and to engage them by connecting academic content, knowledge and skills in transformation projects aligned to community needs. Students can choose where to perform the service experience at a fair where over 70 local organizations communicate different projects.

Resources Required for Success.

The Lánzate Center for Leadership Development.   In 2007, UDEM built the Lánzate Center, a 1,487-square-meter laboratory for the practice of leadership. The center has eleven different rope courses that comply with standards of the Association for Challenge Course Technology (ACCT) including a climbing tower and the Discovery Course, the only challenge course of its kind in Latin America with more than 20 tasks that participants perform at heights of 19 to 49 feet. See Figure 6.3.

Every year the Lánzate Center offers 150 programs tailored to develop specific competences and skills; it serves over 6,600 participants, mainly students of UDEM but also faculty, staff, and corporate personnel from local enterprises. The center coordinates its operation and programs with the Association for Experiential Education, the National Outdoor Leadership School, with Callenge Towers and the ACCT and is operated by a team of five professionals who combine administrative chores with the design and facilitation of leadership programs. UDEM promotes the staff's permanent preparation and high-level training in the areas of group facilitation, technical details of the challenge courses, adventure programming, risk management, and first aid, as well as emergency and evacuation protocols.

Figure 6.3. Lánzate Center

Safety is a priority at the center. The rope courses are subject to frequent inspections and maintenance, participants always engage in a challenge by choice and submit personal emergency contacts, medical and insurance information prior to the program.

Results.   Is UDEM succeeding in its goal of educating transformational leaders? Seeking to assess the institution's efforts UDEM has participated in the Multi-Institutional Study of Leadership (MSL; 2015), an international research program that seeks to understand the influence of higher education in promoting leadership development. The theoretical framework of the MSL, the Social Change Model of Leadership Development, involves social responsibility and change as core principles and analyzes core values that resonate with UDEM's leadership development model (Higher Education Research Institute [HERI], 1996); the conceptual framework for the research is based on Astin's (1993) input-environments-outcomes college impact model.

Results for 2015 show that UDEM's students scored above the United States national benchmark on all the values of the Social Change Model (MSL, 2015); the community service experience and involvement in college organizations influence the study's outcome measures. Students report a significant positive difference between precollege and senior year experiences on six variables, including consciousness of self, commitment, and collaboration revealing the impact of the university's educational model.

Challenges, Future Directions, and Recommendations

UDEM continues to enhance its educational offerings and seeks to respond to the urgent needs of the national context. In 2015, the model was innovated to incorporate integrity, sustainability, and intercultural competence as core themes in addition to citizenship and social responsibility. The challenges ahead in the operation of the model include permanent training of staff, creating opportunities for faculty to engage and communicating its benefits both for students and the institution. Some positive indicators on the work of the Universidad de Monterrey are the sustained growth in enrollment for the past four years, the positive feedback from employers and alumni as well as results in the MSL.

References

Astin, A. W. (1993). *What matters in college: Four critical years revisited.* San Francisco, CA: Jossey-Bass.

Builes Jaramillo, J. F. (2003). *El abordaje de la educación experiencial.* Bogotá, Colombia: QuickPress.

Burns, J. M. (1978). *Leadership.* New York, NY: Harper & Row.

Cantón, A. (2011). *How institutional contexts influence the civic development of students at three Mexican universities.* (Doctoral thesis). Available from ProQuest Dissertations and Theses Database. (UMI No. 3455404).

Esquivel, G. (2015). *Desigualdad extrema en México, concentración del poder económico y político* (p. 44). Mexico, DF: OXFAM México.

Hayes, S., Galvan, J., & Del Castillo, A. (2008). *Encuesta de fraude y corrupción en México 2008.* México, D.F.: KPMG en México.

Higher Education Research Institute [HERI]. (1996). *A social change model of leadership development: Guidebook version III.* College Park, MD: National Clearinghouse for Leadership Programs.

Komives, S. R., Lucas, N., & McMahon, T. R. (1998). *Exploring leadership. For college students who want to make a difference.* San Francisco, CA: Jossey-Bass.

Luckner, J., & Nadler, R. (1997). *Processing the experience. Strategies to enhance and generalize learning* (2nd ed.). Dubuque, IA: Kendall/Hunt.

Multi-Institutional Study of Leadership. (2015). *2015 School report general and sub-study outcomes.* Monterrey, Mexico: Universidad de Monterrey.

O'Donnell, G. (1997). *Contrapuntos. Ensayos escogidos sobre autoritarismo y demogratización.* Buenos Aires, Argentina: Editorial Paidós.

Organisation for Economic Co-operation and Development. (2014). *Mexico. Education at a glance: OECD indicators.* Paris, France: Author.

Organization for Economic Co-operation and Development. (2007). *Education at a glance 2007.* Paris, France: Author.

Programa de las Naciones Unidas para el Desarrollo. (2004). *La Democracia en América Latina. Hacia una democracia de ciudadanos y ciudadanas.* Buenos Aires, Argentina: Author.

Secretaría de Gobernación. (2012). *Encuesta nacional sobre cultura política y prácticas ciudadanas 2012.* Retrieved from http://encup.gob.mx/work/models/Encup/Resource/69/1/images/Presentacion-Quinta-ENCUP-2012.pdf

Solt, F. (2014). *The standardized world income inequality database.* Retrieved from http://myweb.uiowa.edu/fsolt/swiid/swiid.html

Transparency International. (2013). *"Mexico" global corruption barometer.* Retrieved from http://www.transparency.org/gcb2013/country/?country=mexico

Transparency International. (2014). *Corruption perception index.* Retrieved from http://www.transparency.org/research/cpi/overview

UNESCO. (2016). *The four pillars of learning*. Retrieved from http://www.unesco.org/n ew/en/education/networks/global-networks/aspnet/about-us/strategy/the-four-pillars -of-learning/

United Nations Development Programme. (2010). *MDG Progress reports—Latin America and the Caribbean*. Retrieved from http://www.undp.org/content/undp/en/home /librarypage/mdg/mdg-reports/lac-collection.html

World Bank. (2015). *Country Brief: Mexico*. Retrieved from http://data.worldbank.org /country/mexico#cp_wdi

Yukl, G. A. (1994). *Leadership in organizations* (3rd ed.). Englewood Cliffs, NJ: Prentice Hall.

ALICIA CANTÓN is director of student affairs at UDEM with 15 years of experience in higher education. She received her doctorate in higher education administration from the University of Pennsylvania. She has served as Mexico's representative for NASPA's Latin America and the Caribbean region and southeastern division.

NEW DIRECTIONS FOR HIGHER EDUCATION • DOI: 10.1002/he

7

This chapter reviews models, theories, and cross-national data on student learning and development and explores these within their context.

Promoting Student Learning and Development

Ellen M. Broido, Birgit Schreiber

The examples of practice from South Africa, China, the United Kingdom, and Mexico in Chapters 3 through 6 of this volume demonstrate the importance of carefully considering aspects of the individual, community, and country when designing initiatives to enhance student learning and development. Before beginning our overview of student learning and development, we invite readers to consider their informal theories of student change, including how undergraduate students develop and what facilitates that development (Knefelkamp, Widick, & Parker, 1978). Given variation in the range of higher education outcomes across institutions, the nation and the world, what student development and learning theory is salient?

How students are engaged, taught, and encouraged to learn and develop reflects the cultural and national contexts in which they were raised and in which they currently find themselves, which may or may not be congruent with their cultures of origin. Those cultural contexts vary within and across national borders, and depend on national and regional narratives, norms, and socio-cultural as well as economic–political agendas.

However, most research on student learning and development in higher education arose within the United States, and reflects hegemonic assumptions and values held by researchers, students, and institutions. In this chapter, we broaden the perspective, to the extent possible given existing literature, to consider ways undergraduate students' learning and development are similar and diverge across national and socio-cultural contexts. We utilize a social justice perspective, presuming students have the right to appropriate and effective education that respects their identities and backgrounds; that is culturally, nationally, and internationally relevant; and that equips students to recognize and challenge structural and societal barriers to equitable opportunities for all.

New Directions for Higher Education, no. 175, Fall 2016 © 2016 Wiley Periodicals, Inc.
Published online in Wiley Online Library (wileyonlinelibrary.com) • DOI: 10.1002/he.20200

Concepts and Contexts

We view all aspects of development as interdependent, seeing social-personal-emotional development and academic-cognitive progress as "inextricably intertwined" (King & Baxter Magolda, 1996, p. 163), with both essential to mastery of higher-education outcomes. We believe any separation between learning and development is reductionist, artificial, and a divorce of development from context.

Concepts of learning and development reflect various regional and national agendas and discourses into which higher education is embedded (Schreiber, 2013). Student learning and development depend both on the context of higher education and on the wider socio-political national context into which postsecondary institutions are embedded (see Chapter 8 in this volume). When higher education operates within a social welfare state, student support and development are largely community driven, embedded into the wider social sphere and managed by the state. A useful example is the *Studentenwerk* in Germany, which is a state-funded organization using community embedded systems to support and develop students (www.studentenwerke.de/en/node/61). Where higher education is considered a tool within reconstruction of the social–economic fabric of society, development is aligned with national development agendas, much like in southern Africa (www.sadc.int). Some developmental theories emphasize infusion and articulation. For example, at Australia's Victoria University, student development is "concerned with both their campus-based experiences but also the larger ways education features in their lives" (Funston, Gil, & Gilmore, 2014, p. 1) and takes a "whole-of-institution approach" (p. 3).

Some institutions rely on in- and out-of class contexts for student development, utilizing student organizations, on-campus jobs, residence halls, student governance, sports, as well as classrooms, labs, and studios as developmental environments. Additionally, student learning and development can be fostered in authentic pedagogies focusing on experiential learning, real-world immersion, and reflection, recognizing that development is not discrete but a continuous process across students' lives (Jackson, 2010).

Social Justice Frameworks for Student Learning and Development

UNESCO's World Declaration on Higher Education for the Twenty-first Century (1998) called on higher education institutions worldwide to address issues of access and equity and how student development has evolved to embrace these principles of social justice. According to Castells (2009), the university provides many functions for societies, and although it legitimizes certain elites via knowledge production, it also has become a "social equaliser" that provides opportunity for broad development and social mobility and thus has become a key player in the social–economic advancement of national transformation agendas (Cloete & Maassen, 2015, p. 3). This is particularly pronounced in the emerging economies where higher education is a pathway for social mobility and student development theories reflect the social justice agenda into which higher education is, in part, embedded. According to Osei-Kofi (2011), shaping student development to reflect principles of social justice is essential so as to, firstly, transform the university and society's invisible, discursive, and systemic structures and practices that maintain positionality and privilege; and, secondly, to enable students to challenge the hegemony of inequitable societal practices.

Fraser's (2009) concept of participatory parity centers on creating opportunities to enable an equitable chance of participation in all aspects of higher education and society. This transformative approach questions the invisible social structures and pervasive practices that maintain inequities. Universal Design for Learning (Burgstahler, 2015) promotes flexible approaches to learning and development via multiple ways of representation and expression of learning and development, thus broadening access by accommodating multiple engagement styles (Schreiber, 2013).

Student Development Theories

Development refers to "the ways that a student grows, progresses, or increases his or her developmental capabilities as a result of enrollment in an institution of higher education" (Rogers, 1990, p. 27). Theories of student learning and development presume growth is a consequence of interaction between the person and the environment (Lewin, 1936). Development is the consequence of both individual readiness and appropriately supportive environments (i.e., slightly more support than challenge; Evans, Forney, Guido, Patton, & Renn, 2009; Sanford, 1966). Particularly for first generation or nontraditional students and for those universities that engage these students, understanding student-context is essential. Otherwise, students may be forced to "shed parts of themselves" (Funston et al., 2014, p. 21) in the process of transitioning into and developing graduate attributes that are relevant not only within higher education but within their wider life experience. Institutions must adapt to meet the needs of these students rather than relying solely on students to change (Funston et al., 2014).

Identity Development. There is increasing international recognition of the need to attend to students' identity development in multiple aspects, including career, interpersonal, and cultural domains. Although utilized extensively in the United States, identity-development models have been criticized for prioritizing autonomy, self-direction, and activism, predominant values in Western cultures, but less emphasized in some other parts of the world.

Personal Identity. Building on the work of Erikson (1959/1980), models of personal identity reflect changes in how people understand "their unique ways of being" (Chickering & Reisser, 1993, p. 35), their relationships with others, and commitments they make to their communities. Models of personal identity development address students' understandings of their values, purpose, their relationships with family and significant others, the development of competence and effective interpersonal relationships, among other aspects.

Most research on personal identity has been done in the United States and Canada, with recent growth in Europe (Schwartz, Zanboanga, Meca, & Ritchie, 2012). Schwartz et al. (2012) noted "the *structure* of identity development is similar across [European and the United States] countries but ... identity processes (i.e., forms of exploration and commitment) are endorsed to different extents between and among countries" (p. 8, italics in original) because of different cultural contexts. They also noted that the still-limited research done in East Asia shows "that structure of personal identity is not equivalent between American and East Asian young people" (p. 8). Specifically, East Asian concepts of self are more expansive than Western notions, including family members, and identity may be developed more through "imitation and identification" (p. 9) than through exploration.

Social–Cultural Identity.   Social or cultural identity development foregrounds a person's attachment to and identification with a culture or group. In some regions, notably in Africa and Asia, belonging to and being accepted by a discrete group becomes part of one's self-concept. For contexts in which collective culture plays a significant role in identity, students need to negotiate a sense of belonging to and separating from the collective, being shaped by and simultaneously shaping the collective identity. Social identity constructs like *Ubuntu* ("a person is a person through other people"), where self-concepts are constructed through and via the collective, have received much attention as cultural notions of collective well-being, but are also problematized as marginalizing minoritized students (Marais, 2012).

University students' understandings of the meaning of aspects of their own and others' social identities such as gender, ethnicity, race, nationality, sexual orientation, ability status, and other culturally salient dimensions differ as the meanings of those identities vary widely across contexts. Across many of these models (as developed in the United States) there is a common pattern of movement from acceptance of dominant definitions, through immersion into communities of people sharing those identities and active exploration of alternative understandings of that identity, to a personal, affirmative redefinition of the meaning of that identity and integration of that identity into one's overall self-concept. However, there is no evidence of these models' international applicability.

Universities strive to develop students' ability to move across cultural boundaries (Campbell, 2010); this outcome is particularly important with increasing international mobility, and as students use social media and the Internet to enact their identities across national boundaries. Identity

NEW DIRECTIONS FOR HIGHER EDUCATION • DOI: 10.1002/he

development as a world citizen incorporates awareness of systemic interrelatedness, mutual responsibility, and implication in each other's lives.

Theories of Career Development.   Understandings of work and career, and the need to find meaning and purpose through vocation, transcend nation and culture (Leung, 2008). That said, multiple cross-national differences exist in the influence of work and career on one's self-concept, the range and number of employment opportunities, the extent and importance of choice, and economic context. These aspects contribute to meaningful differences in students' career development and in career development theories. Perhaps notions of "choice," "career," and "fulfillment" are part of middle-class discourse that eludes some regions where any gainful work is a means to reasonable living.

Helping students determine their career interests is a primary driver of career development in the United States, and Holland's (1997) model of career interest remains prevalent. However, Leung (2008) found only "mixed support for Holland's structure of vocational interests across cultures" (p. 119). Leung noted that in some cultures career and work decisions are not individually determined, but collectively shaped. "In order to maximize self-fulfillment and social approval, one has to negotiate with the environment to locate the most acceptable solutions and option" (Leung, 2008, p. 122). Especially when the collective provides funding and support for education, the influence of the collective on career decisions is pronounced.

Developing awareness of career development is itself empowering and may increase a sense of agency within which career narratives and pathways are imagined and developed (Maree, 2013). Maree (2013) argued that career-development theories must incorporate career fluidity and flexibility and recognize that future careers may not yet exist. These aspects of constructivist and narrative career development theories enable students to prepare for a career that requires adaptation, lifelong learning, and re-invention of the self within yet unimagined realities.

Cognitive-Structural Development. Theories of cognitive-structural development describe progressively more adaptive and complex forms of reasoning. Development results from disequilibrium in the environment, when new information cannot be understood within existing meaning-making structures.

Epistemological Development.   Recent theorizing about epistemological development, that is, *how* one understands what can be known, problematizes normative assumptions about the skilled or deficient learner and instead highlights the importance of "learning how to become a successful participant in an academic practice" (Morrow, 2009, p. 77). Hence, active participation in formal education shapes students' access to ways of knowing and learning. Epistemological development is characterized by domain-general and domain-specific epistemic beliefs; some cognitive structures can be generalized across different and cognate fields, whereas other epistemic beliefs remain characteristic of the specific disciplinary thinking.

Epistemological development refers to changes in assumptions about the nature of knowledge, how truth is known and with what certainty, and the role of evidence in making truth claims. In the United States, study of epistemological development in university students began with the work of Perry (1970), and has been refined in the research of multiple later scholars. Across all models, there is progression from understanding knowledge as absolute, static, and held by authorities; through an intermediate stage in which knowledge is perceived as uncertain and claims are idiosyncratic; into a final position in which evaluation of evidence and logic allow for provisional and contextually bound knowledge claims (Evans et al., 2009). Development in these models is hypothesized to be unidirectional in most circumstances, with most university students moving from late in the first stage into the middle stage while attending higher education (King & Baxter Magolda, 1996).

However, patterns of epistemological development (Hofer, 2008) vary across cultures. Weinstock (2010) argued that because engagement in formal education correlates with development, "epistemologies [must] develop consistently with the goals and values of particular cultural activities" (p. 118). In cultures in which challenging authority is discouraged, advanced reasoning may not involve autonomous reasoning, as Western models predict. These forms are not inherently less developed; Hofer reported studies indicating that, although students in Japan, as compared to students in the United States, had less developed beliefs about the nature of knowledge and knowing, they were as academically successful, often exceeding the United States students in assessments of science and math skills.

Hofer (2008) called for additional research into forms of epistemological development in multiple cultures. She noted such research "might lead to the identification of stages and/or dimensions not readily evident in western society" (p. 15) and called for researchers to question what makes different forms of reasoning "sophisticated" in different settings.

Moral Reasoning Development.   Contrasting with other models of development, there is extensive literature regarding the development of moral reasoning across a wide range of nations and cultures (Gibbs, Basinger, Grime, & Snarey, 2007). Although Kohlberg (1981) argued for cultural universality of his model, most international research using his instrumentation found the highest levels of moral reasoning (postconventional) were evident only in groups that were urbanized, economically privileged, and well educated compared to their conationals, arguably because the principles of postconventional reasoning were derived from philosophies presuming interaction with diverse others. Although there were early critiques of gender and cultural bias in Kohlberg's model (Gilligan, 1982), that finding was overturned upon review of his data. Most contemporary measures, both within the United States and cross-nationally, find women score slightly higher than men on Kohlberg's instruments (Gibbs et al., 2007). Contemporary research assessing the development of moral reasoning in a more culturally neutral way, while limited by cross-sectional rather than longitudinal designs, demonstrates cross-national gains in moral reasoning with aging, urbanicity, and advanced education, likely because of enhanced opportunities for taking social perspective (Gibbs et al., 2007). Thus, university efforts to expand contact with diverse others and expand perspective taking may enhance the development of moral reasoning.

Religiosity and ethical ideologies are important in the development of moral reasoning. Some research suggests that religiosity, especially reliance on dogma, correlates with preference for order and structure, predictability and conformity with authority, and a discomfort with ambivalences and paradoxes (Duriez, 2003). Higher-level spirituality, including the search for truth and questioning one's faith, correlate with Kohlberg's higher levels of moral reasoning, suggesting that not religion in itself, but a construct underpinning religiosity, influences morality.

Self-Authorship.   Baxter Magolda (2010), building on the work of Kegan (1994), defined self-authorship as the point in development in which "the internal capacity to generate and manage one's beliefs, identity, and social relations emerged" (p. 267), thus requiring development in the intertwined domains of epistemology, personal identity, and interpersonal relationships. Although self-authorship rarely is achieved as an undergraduate student (Evans et al., 2009), it is critical for effective functioning in an increasingly complex, interconnected world (Kegan, 1994). Kegan (as reported in Baxter Magolda, 2010), believed self-authorship was possible in both individually focused and collective contexts and that "it is possible to go through all the constructive-developmental stages in a connected way or a separate way" (Baxter Magolda, 2010, p. 269). Thus, self-authored individuals in collective cultures can individually generate their own sense of selves and beliefs if they do not require shared beliefs to stay in relationship with people, because "the nature of the connection isn't predicated on ... having the same view" (p. 270). Baxter Magolda called for further research examining "the extent to which the internal authority of self-authoring, with its capacity to coordinate external expectations, can be shaped around interdependence and authentic relationships rather than around autonomy" (p. 275).

Implications for Practice

Student learning and development are neither discrete nor isolated events. Learning and development are deeply contextualized and embedded into national narratives and socio-political discourses. Moreover, development and learning are complex processes across the holistic spectrum of cognitive-epistemological, intra- and interpersonal aspects of students' identities and lives, constructed and reconstructed in alignment with the world in which they live.

We hope this chapter contributed toward the awareness of personal and systemic notions and practices that advance student learning and development in ways that promote social justice. We encourage readers from across the world to contribute to future research on undergraduate students' learning and development and to help expand understanding of patterns of similarity and uniqueness across contexts and regions in students' growth.

References

Baxter Magolda, M. B. (2010). Future directions: Pursuing theoretical and methodological issues in the evolution of self-authorship. In M. B. Baxter Magolda, E. G. Creamer, & P. S. Meszaros (Eds.), *Development and assessment of self-authorship: Exploring the concept across cultures* (pp. 267–284). Sterling, VA: Stylus.

Burgstahler, S. E. (2015). *Universal design in higher education: From principle to practice* (2nd ed.). Cambridge, MA: Harvard University Press.

Campbell, A. (2010). Cultural identity as a social construct. *Intercultural Education, 11*(1), 31–39. doi:10.1080/14675980050005370

Castells, M. (2009). *Transcript from a lecture on the role of universities in development, the economy and society.* University of the Western Cape, South Africa. Retrieved from www.uchile.cl/documentos/lecture-on-higher-education_113390_49_1026.pdf

Chickering, A. W., & Reisser, L. (1993). *Education and identity* (2nd ed.). San Francisco, CA: Jossey-Bass.

Cloete, N., & Maassen, P. (2015). Roles of universities and the African context. In N. Cloete, P. Maassen, & T. Bailey (Eds.), *Knowledge production: Contradictory functions in African higher education,* (pp. 75–108). Cape Town, South Africa: African Minds.

Duriez, B. (2003). Vivisecting the religious mind: Religiosity and motivated social cognition. *Mental Health, Religion, & Culture, 6,* 79–86.

Erikson, E. H. (1980). *Identity and the life cycle.* New York, NY: Norton. (Original work published 1959)

Evans, N. J., Forney, D. S., Guido, F. M., Patton, L D., & Renn, K. A. (2009). *Student development in college* (2nd ed.). San Francisco, CA: Jossey-Bass.

Fraser, N. (2009). *Scales of justice. Reimagining justice in a globalising world.* New York, NY: Columbia University Press.

Funston, A., Gil, M., & Gilmore, G. (2014). Supporting students' transitions in challenging times. In A. Funston, M. Gil, & G. Gilmore (Eds.), *Strong starts, supported transitions, and student success* (pp. 1–30). New Castle, England: Cambridge Scholars.

Gibbs, J. C., Basinger, K. S., Grime, R. L., & Snarey, J. R. (2007). Moral judgment development across cultures: Revisiting Kohlberg's universality claims. *Developmental Review, 27,* 443–500.

Gilligan, C. (1982). *In a different voice: Psychological theory and women's development.* Cambridge, MA: Harvard University Press.

Hofer, B. K. (2008). Personal epistemology and culture. In M. Khine (Ed.), *Knowing, knowledge and beliefs* (pp. 3–22). Dordrecht, The Netherlands: Springer.

Holland, J. H. (1997). *Making vocational choices: A theory of vocational personalities and work environments* (3rd ed.). Englewood Cliffs, NJ: Prentice-Hall.

Jackson, N. (2010). From a curriculum that integrates work to a curriculum that integrates life: Changing a university's conceptions of curriculum. *Higher Education Research & Development, 29*(5), 491–505. doi:10.1080/07294360.2010.502218

Kegan, R. (1994). *In over our heads: The mental demands of modern life*. Cambridge, MA: Harvard University Press.

King, P. M., & Baxter Magolda, M. B. (1996). A developmental perspective on learning. *Journal of College Student Development, 37*, 163–173.

Knefelkamp, L., Widick, C., & Parker, C. (1978). Editors' notes: Why bother with theory? In L. Knefelkamp, C. Widick, & C. Parker (Eds.), *Applying new developmental findings* (New Directions for Student Services, no. 4, pp. vii–xvi). San Francisco, CA: Jossey-Bass.

Kohlberg, L. (1981). *Essays on moral development: Vol. I. The philosophy of moral development*. San Francisco, CA: Harper & Row.

Lewin, K. (1936). *Principles of typological psychology*. New York, NY: McGraw-Hill.

Leung, S. A. (2008). The big five career theories. In J. A. Athanasou, & R. Van Esbroeck (Eds.), *International handbook of career guidance* (pp. 115–132) [ebook]. New York, NY: Springer. doi:10.1007/978-1-4020-6230-8

Marais, B. (2012). *Queering Ubuntu: The self and the other in South African queer autobiography* (Master's thesis, University of KwaZulu-Natal). Retrieved from www.genderlinks.org.za/attachment.php?aa_id=17681

Maree, J. G. (2013). *Counselling for career construction*. Rotterdam, Netherlands: Sense.

Morrow, W. (2009). *Bounds of democracy: Epistemological access to higher education*. Pretoria, South Africa: HSRC.

Osei-Kofi, N. (2011). Beyond awareness: Student affairs educators as social justice advocates. In P. M. Magolda, & M. B. Baxter Magolda (Eds.), *Contested issues in student affairs* (pp. 387–392). Sterling, VA: Stylus.

Perry, W. G. (1970). *Forms of intellectual development in the college years*. New York, NY: Holt.

Rogers, R. F. (1990). Student development. In U. Delworth, G. R. Hanson, & Associates, *Student services: A handbook for the profession* (2nd ed., pp. 117–164). San Francisco, CA: Jossey-Bass.

Sanford, N. (1966). *Self and society*. New York, NY: Atherton.

Schreiber, B. (2013). Constructions of students as client or partner in knowledge creation? *Journal of Psychology in Africa, 23*(4), 85–89.

Schwartz, S. J., Zamboanga, B. L., Meca, A., & Ritchie, R. A. (2012). Identity around the world: An overview. In S. J. Schwartz (Ed.), *Identity around the world* (New Directions for Child and Adolescent Development, no. 138, pp. 1–18). San Francisco, CA: Jossey-Bass.

UNESCO. (1998). *World declaration on higher education for the twenty-first century*. Retrieved from http://www.unesco.org/education/educprog/wche/declaration_eng.htm

Weinstock, M. (2010). Epistemological development of Bedouins and Jews in Israel: Implications for self-authorship. In M. B. Baxter Magolda, E. G. Creamer, & P. S. Meszaros (Eds.), *Development and assessment of self-authorship: Exploring the concept across cultures* (pp. 117–132). Sterling, VA: Stylus.

ELLEN M. BROIDO is an associate professor of higher education and student affairs at Bowling Green State University, United States. Dr. Broido's research focuses on social justice issues in higher education. She is a board member of ACPA: College Student Educators International, and has served as editor of its Books and Media board.

BIRGIT SCHREIBER is the senior director of student affairs at the University of Stellenbosch, South Africa. She has published and presented widely and was a visiting scholar at Berkeley, Oslo, and Leuven universities. She is a board member of the Journal for Student Affairs in Africa, the International Association for Student Affairs/Student Services (IASAS) and NASPA: Student Affairs Administrators in Higher Education.

NEW DIRECTIONS FOR HIGHER EDUCATION • DOI: 10.1002/he

8

This chapter explores students interacting in their environments, specifically the influence of culture in student learning and development. Cultural applications in Singapore are featured.

Student and Community Characteristics

Susan R. Komives, Teck Koon Tan

Learning and development happens in a context that is shaped by the values of importance to those in the culture. Culture is widely understood to add meaning to the shared experience through the ideas, social structures, art, morals, and religious beliefs that are directly and indirectly taught and transmitted among a group of people (Griswold, 1994). Understanding the role of key dimensions of a nation and local community as well as the role of the family, religion, and social identity enhances a critical perspective on designing appropriate strategies for student learning and development. As noted in Chapter 1 of this volume, "It is essential ... to adopt a critical perspective to evaluate the appropriateness of any given cross-border internationalization strategy for student learning and development, resulting in a conclusion to transfer, adapt, hedge, or avoid the practice." This chapter will explore frameworks useful in understanding culture and its role in shaping learning and developmental contexts with examples from Singapore as illustrations.

Cultural Context

Ecological models of social learning theory have long asserted that individual and group behavior is a function of the person(s) interacting with the environment. Lewin's (1951) heuristic equation for this phenomena is $B = f(P, E)$. Using a cultural lens to inform the environment dimension of this concept is crucial.

The complexity of international cultures has intrigued those who engage in cross-border work for many years and have become more critical in the internationalization of higher education. Both Hofstede's classic work (2001; Hofstede, Hofstede, & Minkov, 2010) and the GLOBE Studies (House, Hanges, Javidan, Dorfman, & Gupta, 2004) provide useful elements to explore in understanding specific dimensions of global cultures. Historic attempts at predictive cultural models have been useful

New Directions for Higher Education, no. 175, Fall 2016 © 2016 Wiley Periodicals, Inc.
Published online in Wiley Online Library (wileyonlinelibrary.com) • DOI: 10.1002/he.20201

but ultimately cannot be relied on for proscriptive applications particularly when applied to individuals. Indeed, Matsumoto (1996) observed, "Our failure in the past to recognize the existence of individual differences in constructs and concepts of culture has undoubtedly aided in the formation and maintenance of stereotypes" (p. 18). At best, those models help us understand group aggregates.

Bronfenbrenner's Social–Ecological Model. Russian American developmental psychologist Urie Bronfenbrenner's (1979) ecological framework for human development is one of the most useful in analyzing student learners in their own cultural context. Historically, this model applied sociological process perspectives to human development, initially to child development, and is presented as concentric circles with the individual in the center showing levels, or systems, of influence on that individual. From the inner most circle, these system levels are the (1) *Microsystem* that includes the most immediate and direct influences (that is, proximal) on a student's development like the family, neighborhood, school, peers, and religion institutions. (2) The next level, the *Mesosystem,* incorporates the interactions among elements of the microsystem (like peers in school). (3) The next level is the *Exosystem* that involves interactions between the individual's immediate context and social settings that the individual is not involved with, like how the experience at school may be influenced by administrative budget cuts. (4) The *Macrosystem* is the larger culture in which all elements exist including heritage and whether located in industrialized or developing countries. Macrosystems evolve over time as illustrated by the rapid change in some Middle Eastern cultures moving from nomadic orientations to the creation of elaborate, wealthy cities or the changes in the implementation of communism in China. (5) The final level is the *Chronosystem* that examines changes over time in the life course like the role of divorce in a family or applications of technology.

Bronfenbrenner (1989; Tudge, Mokrova, Hatfield, & Karnik, 2009) expanded his systems model to include processes of human development; hence the model is now viewed as the Process-Person-Context-Time Model (PPCT). (1) *Processes* are central and most powerful to human development—particularly those closest or proximal. Direct engagement by the student with others and with learning experiences make the biggest impact on growth. (2) Bronfenbrenner describes three aspects of the *person* as "demand" characteristics (observable dimensions like age or gender that may influence interactions); "resource" characteristics (intrapersonal assets like intelligence, emotional strength, or experience as well as material resources such as family status or nutrition); and "force" characteristics (motivation, commitment, persistence) that may explain how some students with similar "demand" and "resource" characteristics have different outcomes. (3) The *context* includes the four levels of systems in the original theory: the microsystem, mesosystem, exosystem, and macrosystem. (4) The final element of *Time* is viewed as micro-time (what is happening in the here and now), meso-time (the effect of events that influence the student occurring with consistency), and macro-time (the life span of the chronosystem). As an ecological model, Bronfenbrenner's early work was critiqued as focused predominately on the context or environment so the PPCT model incorporated more dimensions of the person (Tudge et al., 2009). For our purposes, the context is largely the dimension of cultural analysis. Bronfenbrenner's model is perhaps most useful in analyzing cultural contexts.

Central Cultural Domains. Bronfenbrenner's model (1979, 1989) poses a contextual framework for useful questions (See Table 8.1) to explore in promoting culturally appropriate decisions leading to original program design as well as decisions on whether to transfer, adapt, hedge, or avoid practices and programs from other cultures or in designing experiences within a culture. Key elements of the role of personal and social identity, family, religion, and place make it clearer, for example, that Western coeducational housing options would not transfer (and should be avoided) in cultures where religious, gender, and family expectations value separation of the sexes. Likewise, expectations of chaperones accompanying young women may be adapted from Middle Eastern to Western institutions where those youth are young, in high-risk situations, or in culturally novel environments. Family orientation programs may be of high interest and transfer well to the Middle East where the collectivist cultural role of the family is preeminent.

Singapore Context

A useful example of an educational system that illustrates these dimensions is that of Singapore. Singapore's success in education is highly acknowledged worldwide (OECD, 2011), as are its universities; the National University of Singapore (NUS) was ranked 26th in the world and first in Asia (Times Higher Education World University Rankings, 2016). The evolution of the Singapore education system is comprehensively documented (Deng, Gopinathan, & Lee, 2013; Lee, Goh, Fredriksen, & Tan, 2008). The Singapore example illustrates the cultural influences on student learning and development as the country progressed, how these influences contributed to the success of the education system as well as to gaps that limit the learning process, and how institutions attempt to realign student learning and development, through education reforms, to the needs of the 21st century.

An Ecological Systems View in Singapore. Formal education is highly valued in the macrosystem and people place a premium on formal education. This is evident in the microsystem: families have high hopes and expectations of their children attaining the highest level of education possible and this typically and traditionally alludes to a university education, although the mindset has changed to consider other educational pathways such as vocational institutes and polytechnics. This shared macrosystem philosophy and goal has contributed to the ease and remarkable pace

NEW DIRECTIONS FOR HIGHER EDUCATION • DOI: 10.1002/he

Table 8.1. Sample Cultural Questions Derived from Bronfenbrenner's Model

System	Element/Description	Example/Questions
Microsystem	Role of the person and social identity	How pervasive are gender roles and gender expectations/equity?
		What helpful norms are related to race, ethnicity, or nationality?
		How are personal aspects such as sexual orientation or socioeconomic status approached in the culture?
		How do multiple identities function, that is, intersectionality (e.g., being a Muslim woman in a Middle Eastern Islamic country versus in a Western University)
	Role of family	Is this a collectivist or individualist culture?
		What role have students played in the family during high school?
	Role of religion	Do individuals make a personal choice about their religion, is it family-based, or is it a predominant national practice?
		How closely is the person expected to practice religious tenants?
		How frequently is religious worship practiced (e.g., daily)?
Mesosystem	Interactions within the microsystem	What do families expect of the university?
		How do peers interact while at university?
		How do religious practices influence university life?
		What aspects of the person and social identities are salient in university life?
		What is the nature of student-faculty interactions?
Exosystem	Local community	How does the location of the university (e.g., rural, city) influence learning?
		What are considered good practices by university educators in this region or nation?
Macrosystem	Nation	How does the governmental system influence individual life and learning?
		What are expectations regarding deference to hierarchy or authority?
		Is there a dominant national religion?
		Are there vestiges of colonialism that make adaptation difficult or even suspect?
		What role does the university (higher or tertiary education) play in public policy?
Chronosystem	Changes over time	How have national changes (e.g., economy, war, gender roles) influenced other systems?
		How are attitudes toward youth changing over time?

NEW DIRECTIONS FOR HIGHER EDUCATION • DOI: 10.1002/he

with which education has made tremendous progress and advancement in Singapore.

As individuals in the microsystem, Singaporean students are hard-working and generally want to do well in their studies. There are various microsystem reasons, or "forces," for this—the desire to meet collectivistic parental expectations and aspirations, and sibling pressure; competition and peer pressure; self-motivation; and personal aspiration. Although religion is important and relevant to a large segment of the Singaporean community with Christianity, Buddhism, Islam, Hinduism, and Taoism constituting the major faiths, it has less direct or visible impact on the pursuit of formal education at the household, community, or national level since 97% of Singaporean children are enrolled in the secular national school system.

Cultural Factors Influencing a Desire for Formal Education in Singapore.   Several factors are critical in understanding the high regard for formal education. Examples from Bronfenbrenner's systems illustrate these cultural factors.

The Family Factor (Microsystem).   One aspect of the family factor is the strong desire of families to break the poverty chain. At the time of independence (1965), the Singapore community was a diaspora of the very wealthy and the very poor. Families placed a premium on their children getting a formal education as a way to break out of poverty. The aspiration was a university degree, seen as the passport to a career and better life. In particular, parents aspired for their children to be recruited into the premier white-collar civil service or graduate as a doctor or engineer.

Admission to universities is highly competitive, requiring sterling academic grades. Hence, students focus on studying to obtain top academic entry grades. Families provide strong support and "push," often investing financially (like hiring private tutors to provide additional coaching to their children at the primary and secondary school levels) to ensure that their children receive the best chance to excel in their studies. The average Singaporean student would have acquired a grade-centric outlook toward education and learning by the time he or she arrives at the university.

Another aspect of family influence on learning is ethno-cultural. About 74% of the Singapore population is made up of ethnic Chinese whose philosophy on deference for authority, including elders and teachers, may be traced to a Confucian root. The reticence among many students in classrooms could be attributed to this (not wanting to appear "outspoken," "challenging," "too smart," or disrespectful); or simply to the desire to avoid making mistakes and thus "losing face" (loss of pride) before their peers. Whatever the reason, learning becomes unidirectional and teacher centered. Precepts are not challenged, thus compromising on active learning and creative thinking. Although this mindset is changing among the more individualistic and contemporary youth, the reticence to speak up and to openly participate in classroom discussions is still evident among students today.

NEW DIRECTIONS FOR HIGHER EDUCATION • DOI: 10.1002/he

The Community Factor (Exosystem and Mesosystem). The strong financial support (grants, subsidies, bursaries, scholarships) for education provides all segments of the community access to formal education, which brings about career opportunities and social mobility. The acute awareness among families of one's social mobility and social identity, vis-a-vis that of others in the community as the country prospers, plays an influential role in reinforcing the desire for formal education and serves as a multiplier factor across the population.

The Nation Factor (Macrosystem). Postindependence Singapore (1965) focused on nation building through urban development, industrialization, and institutionalizing a strong civil service. From the onset, meritocracy was the "national ideology"—it was emphasized, recognized, and used as the yardstick for admission to schools and institutions of higher learning, job offers, job promotions, and career progression. The decades of focus on meritocracy has evolved a culture that places a premium on examinations and academic grades as the benchmark of one's ability, achievements, and success in education and learning (Wielemans & Chan, 1992). In a way, this resonates with family and community pride within the mesosystem culture. However, the key contemporary concern is that the single-minded pursuit of academic grades eclipses the role that education has in developing the whole person. There are concerns that students would not develop other life skills and personal attributes that are critical to the 21st-century work force. Despite attempts made to defocus on examinations and grades, the issue continues as a matter of concern (Ministry of Education, 2013; UNESCO, 2014).

Addressing the Cultural Factors. Employers' feedback gathered by the NUS Centre for Future-ready Graduates acknowledges that although NUS graduates are highly employable because they are hardworking and informed in their domain knowledge and skills (this may be an outcome of the cultural pragmatic or grade-centric approach toward learning), they often lack other interpersonal and life skills that employers are increasingly expecting of their recruits. To prepare its students for the future, the NUS leadership initiated various educational and curricular reforms including the following:

1. *Mitigating the cultural obsession with examinations and grades to encourage holistic and creative teaching and learning, and measurements of educational outcomes.* Examples of initiatives include the discretionary admissions of freshmen who have demonstrated passion and achievements in areas such as arts and culture, sports, or community service, apart from a minimum level of academic merit; different modes of assessment, such as continual assessment, to encourage continual and progressive learning; the "S/U"(Satisfactory/Unsatisfactory) option that allows students to discount certain poor grades toward the final cumulative average point (equivalent of GPA), to encourage students

NEW DIRECTIONS FOR HIGHER EDUCATION • DOI: 10.1002/he

to be more adventurous toward learning, rather than choosing modules based on perceived ease/difficulty in scoring good grades; and the grade-free freshmen semester to remove the pre-occupation with grades and encourage students to explore their passion for learning.

These changes did not come without apprehension. Faculties were initially concerned that the measures would compromise academic standards and integrity. Students were also initially skeptical about the lesser emphasis on academic grades. Close tracking, however, has shown that students' study behavior has changed for the better, whereas academic rigor and academic attainment have not been compromised. This has allayed the initial misgivings and reservations to change.

2. *Enhancing global exposure and immersion.* NUS established six NUS Overseas Colleges (NOCs) in entrepreneurial hubs in Beijing, Shanghai, Stockholm, Silicon Valley, New York, and Israel to allow its students to immerse in start-ups while reading courses at its top partner universities in the host cities. Other NUS students embark on student exchanges with some 300 top universities in the United States, Europe, and Asia. Students develop cross-cultural skills, and widen and deepen their understanding of world issues through these programs. Employers have been quick to recognize and incorporate this trait in their recruitment criteria. The positive experience of returning students and their enhanced marketability in job search has convinced others that an extra year or semester spent on a program overseas can be life changing.

3. *Redesigning campus living and learning.* NUS's new Residential Colleges (RCs) bring students from diverse cultures and academic disciplines to live and study together, engage in multidisciplinary programs that focus on Global-Asia issues, and develop intellectually through multidimensional approaches. These encourage open discussion, debate, and advocacy that take students out of their comfort zone and away from the teacher-centered mode of learning. Students have found the RC experience enabling, with the result of their being more confident of handling issues in group and multicultural settings.

4. *Redesigning career guidance and preparation.* The NUS Career Centre was repositioned as the new Centre for Future-ready Graduates (CFG) to equip its students with life skills for the 21st-century workplace and challenges. CFG's programs on personal and interpersonal development coupled with internships, industrial attachments, and student leadership activities provide a holistic and experiential learning approach complementing academic teaching.

5. *Proactive student affairs—promoting student development.* University extracurricular and cocurricular activities (ECA, CCA) present a rich resource for student learning and development "beyond classroom grades," in ways that the academic curriculum alone is unable to

NEW DIRECTIONS FOR HIGHER EDUCATION • DOI: 10.1002/he

provide. The NUS Office of Student Affairs (OSA) goes beyond the traditional service role and actively drives student development through sports, arts and culture, community engagement, and organizational leadership. Student Affairs strongly advocates for students' involvement in ECA/CCA because students often cite academic workload as obstacles or disincentives to being more engaged with the community.

NUS's emphasis on more holistic student development coupled with curricular changes to redefine teaching and learning (and learning outcomes) is gradually changing the grade-centered learning culture. NUS students are loosening up to more adventurous and innovative approaches to learning, valuing international and multicultural exposure, and exhibiting greater confidence in charting their personal growth beyond the academic yardstick. This paradigm shift is made possible through the collective aspiration and commitment of the university management, faculties, employers, alumni, parents, and students, with the support of the Education Ministry.

Guides in Assessing Cultural Dimensions of Learning and Development

The cultural models and examples in this chapter illustrate the considerations required to transfer, adapt, hedge, or avoid practices from other cultures in designing learning and developmental experiences. Educators must always wrestle with the dynamic tension between acknowledging existing culture (what is) and encouraging thoughtful change (what needs to be) in the evolution of people, communities, and nations. The elements of the Bronfenbrenner model become a framework to pose questions to guide cocurricular and curriculum design (see Table 8.1). The key to any decision is *do not assume*. Identify key dimensions of the microculture and ask students how important a dimension may be to them.

References

Bronfenbrenner, I. (1979). *The ecology of human development*. Cambridge, MA: Harvard University Press.

Bronfenbrenner, U. (1989). Ecological systems theory. In R. Vasta (Ed.), *Six theories of child development: Revised formulations and current issues* (pp. 187–250). Greenwich, CT: JAI Press.

Deng, Z., Gopinathan, S., & Lee, K. E. C. (Eds). (2013) *Globalization and the Singapore curriculum: From policy to classroom*. Singapore: Springer.

Griswold, W. (1994). *Cultures and societies in a changing world*. Thousand Oaks, CA: Pine Forge Press.

Hofstede, G. (2001). *Culture's consequences: Comparing values, behaviors, institutions, and organizations across nations* (2nd ed.). Thousand Oaks, CA: Sage.

Hofstede, G., Hofstede, G. J., & Minkov, M. (2010). *Cultures and organizations: Software of the mind* (3rd ed.). New York, NY: McGraw-Hill.

House, R. J., Hanges, P. J., Javidan, M., Dorfman, P. W., & Gupta, V. (Eds.). (2004). *Culture, leadership, and organizations: The GLOBE study of 62 societies*. Thousand Oaks, CA: Sage.

Lee, S. K., Goh, C. B., Fredriksen, B., & Tan, J. P. (Eds.). (2008). *Toward a better future: Education and training for economic development in Singapore since 1965*. Washington, DC: World Bank; Singapore: National Institute of Education (NIE) and Nanyang Technological University.

Lewin, K. (1951). *Field theory in social science*. New York, NY: Harper & Row.

Matsumoto, D. (1996). *Culture and psychology*. Pacific Grove, CA: Brooks/Cole.

Ministry of Education. (2013). *FY 2013 Committee of Supply Debate: 1st Reply by Mr Heng Swee Keat, Minister for Education: Hope – Opportunities For All*. Retrieved from www.moe.gov.sg

Organisation for Economic Co-operation and Development (OECD). (2011). *Strong performers and successful reformers in education: Lessons from PISA for the United States*. Paris, France: Author.

Times Higher Education World University Rankings (2016). Retrieved from http://www.timeshighereducation.co.uk/world-university-rankings

Tudge, J. H. R., Mokrova, I., Hatfield, B. E., & Karnik, R. B. (2009). Uses and misuses of Bronfenbrenner's bioecological theory of human development. *Journal of Family Theory & Review, 1*(4), 198–210.

UNESCO. (2014). *Education for all 2015: National review report*. Singapore: Author.

Wielemans, W., & Chan, P. C. (Eds.). (1992). *Education and culture in industrializing Asia: The interaction between industrialization, cultural identity and education*. Leuven, Belgium: Leuven University Press.

SUSAN R. KOMIVES is professor emerita from the student affairs graduate program at the University of Maryland. She is past president of ACPA: College Student Educators International and the Council for the Advancement of Standards in Higher Education.

TECK KOON TAN is associate professor of biological science at the National University of Singapore and has been Dean of Students since 2003. He is the honorary advisor and former president of the Asia Pacific Student Services Association.

NEW DIRECTIONS FOR HIGHER EDUCATION • DOI: 10.1002/he

9

This chapter explores the best practices and resources for adopting assessment and evaluation strategies and practices across countries.

Assessment, Evaluation, and Research

P. Daniel Chen, Charles Mathies

A quick search of the keyword "assessment and higher education" in the Web of Science database showed 448 published articles in 2015, whereas the same search for the year of 1995 yielded 32 results. It is not an overstatement to say that assessment, along with accountability, have become two of the trendiest terms in 21st-century higher education across the world. In this chapter, we aim to highlight best practices and resources used in adopting assessment, evaluation, and educational research internationally.

Defining Assessment and Evaluation

The terms *assessment* and *evaluation* carry similar meanings but are often used separately in the higher education literature. Merriam-Webster's dictionary (2015) defines assessment as "the act of making a judgment about something." Within higher education though, the term *assessment* usually refers to an ongoing process of establishing learning goals, providing learning opportunities to the students, systematically collecting and analyzing evidence to determine how well students learned, and using the resulting information to improve student learning (Suskie, 2004). The term *evaluation*, on the other hand, is usually used within higher education in the context of program evaluation and is defined as a systematic method of collecting and analyzing questions about a project, policy, or program (U.S. Department of Health and Human Services, 2011) or in a summative way gauging the quality of a practice such as when it is used in teaching evaluation (Chen & Hoshower, 2003). Generally speaking, assessment is learner centered and process oriented, which aims to identify areas where teaching and learning can improve, whereas evaluation is judgmental and arrives at a valuation of performance. It should be noted, however, that both terms have been used interchangeably in a wide range of contexts and it is sometimes very difficult to differentiate the meaning of assessment and evaluation.

Ewell (2002) pointed out that there were two dichotomous and usually conflicting purposes of assessment, which were improvement and accountability. In most educational literature, assessment was a means to

NEW DIRECTIONS FOR HIGHER EDUCATION, no. 175, Fall 2016 © 2016 Wiley Periodicals, Inc.
Published online in Wiley Online Library (wileyonlinelibrary.com) • DOI: 10.1002/he.20202

improve student learning by way of appraising an individual's mastery of learning goals and by providing opportunities to develop and grow. However, assessment has also been used to describe large-scale standardized tests or surveys that were used to benchmark the performance of an individual, institution, or country in the name of accountability. This usage happens mostly in the elementary and secondary education context, with one example being the Organisation for Economic Co-operation and Development's (OECD) Programme for International Student Assessment (PISA). However, over the last decade, more and more institutions utilized standardized tests such as Collegiate Learning Assessment (CLA) (Bennett & Wilezol, 2013) or large-scale surveys such as the National Survey of Student Engagement (NSSE) as evidence of student learning and institutional accountability (Kuh, 2003). When assessment is used as an indicator of accountability, it can lose the connotation of improvement and instead focuses on summative quality assurance and judgment.

From the improvement perspective, assessment can also be utilized in two different ways. First, an assessment can be employed to provide personalized learning assistance to individuals. Examples include career centers using psychological tests to help students identify their career interests or professors using exams to assess students' understanding and to provide feedback for individual improvement. A second way of utilizing assessment is to use it for organizational improvement and change. When assessment is used for organizational change, results of individual assessments are aggregated to provide a picture of the organizational condition. An example is using a survey such as NSSE to gauge the level of student involvement on campus and to make campus-wide programmatic changes. Another example is medical schools using students' medical-board-exam passing rates to inform curriculum decisions.

Assessment and Evaluation in the United States.   Higher education in the United States, as well as in many other countries around the world, enjoyed a long period of growth and prosperity in most of the 20th century without much scrutiny. Higher education in the United States grew exponentially both in enrollment and funding between World War II and the early 1980s (Middaugh, 2010). Alas, no prosperity lasts forever. As Thelin points out (2011), the fast growth in student population also brought more public scrutiny in the 1960s and 1970s to United States institutions. A combination of factors, such as demographic change, political inclination, economic downturns, and a negative perception of college student life—for example, partying, fraternities and sororities—led to steady decline in federal and state funding for higher education starting in the mid-1970s. Along with declining financial supports from federal and state government, policymakers and taxpayers in the United States started to demand more accountability data from colleges and universities. This led to the development of Higher Education General Information Survey (HEGIS) by the United States Department of Education in the 1960s, which later evolved into the Integrated Postsecondary Education Data System (IPEDS) in 1985 (Fuller, 2011). Using IPEDS, the United States Department of Education is able to collect accountability data in areas such as admissions, enrollment, outcome measures, finance, and human resources from almost all United States higher education institutions (U.S. Department of Education, 2015).

As the public called for higher education accountability, most United States institutions were ill-prepared to provide systematic information about fiscal responsibility, student learning, and other crucial indicators of accountability when the trend started in the 1960s. When accountability became a primary focus of federal and state higher education policies, institutions were forced to create infrastructures to respond to the demands for data. Thus, most higher education institutions in the United States gradually established a centralized administrative office in charge of collecting, analyzing, reporting, and disseminating assessment data and results. This led to the professionalization of institutional research (IR) and the establishment of the professional organization, the Association for Institutional Research (AIR), in 1966. Some institutions also have an assessment office in addition to the office of institutional research to help coordinate assessment and evaluation on campus (Richard, 2012).

One sector of higher education that quickly embraced the accountability and assessment movement is the student affairs profession. In the United States, the subject of student affairs is an integrated part of higher education and has been organized as a profession for more than 80 years (Rhatigan, 2009). United States student affairs professionals are proud of being campus educators tasked with promoting student development and learning (Kezar, 2009). However, even after years of effort to establish its value on campus, the view of student affairs as merely service providers persists. As such, student affairs must provide evidence of its value (Upcraft & Schuh, 1996), so a significant amount of resources are spent educating and equipping members of the profession with the knowledge and skills needed to conduct good assessment. These efforts led to the establishment of Council for the Advancement of Standards in Higher Education (CAS) in 1979 and the advancement of assessment and standards in student affairs (Arminio & Creamer, 2004).

Assessment and Evaluation in the International Context. Although there is no true singular unified system, higher education can be viewed as a complex combination of international flows and networks of ideas and practices with national higher education systems shaped by history, law, policy, and funding of the country, whereas individual institutions operate within the local, national, and global context (Marginson, 2006). A number of trends found within United States higher education such as massification, increased use of accountability and assessment measures, and introduction of tuition fees have migrated to other national systems of higher education around the world. For instance, many European and Asian Pacific institutions have recently introduced tuition fees as a way of shifting the cost of higher education from governments and taxpayers to parents and students (Johnstone, Teixeira, Rosa, & Vossensteyn, 2008). In short, as noted in Chapter 2, higher education internationally is becoming more alike with many practices and standards being adopted across borders.

Within Europe, assessment and evaluation has undergone a signifi-cant evolution in recent years. When the Bologna Declaration was first an-nounced in 1999, the term *learning outcomes* was not mentioned. Since then, learning outcome assessment has assumed more and more impor-tance in each revision of the Bologna Process (Adam, 2008) with a num-ber of European-wide organizations focused on assessment and evaluation being established. These organizations include the European Consortium for Accreditation (ECA), the European Association for Quality Assurance (ENQA), and the European Quality Assurance Register for Higher Educa-tion (EQAR). Additionally, European-wide standards, such as the Standards and Guidelines for Quality Assurance in the European Higher Education Area (ESG) were developed in the past decade. The main focus of these or-ganizations and standards are to provide accountability and enhancement of student learning through a common framework of policies, standards, structures, and information infrastructure.

Although higher education in Europe has an agreed set of standards, procedures, and guidelines for assessment and evaluation, there is a large variance in the implementation of these "European" assessment and evalu-ation practices and standards within national ministries and individual in-stitutions. Many national ministries and institutions struggle to adopt and implement the European-wide standards and practices while maintaining their own educational customs and culture. This is a critical issue not just in Europe but in anyplace adopting assessment and evaluation practices and policies across borders. Even though there are similarities in higher educa-tion systems across the world, the significant differences among countries and institutions in their educational cultures and practices needs to be con-sidered and accounted for before incorporating ideas and practices across borders (Mathies, 2015).

Another important consideration in adopting assessment and evalua-tion across borders is the influence of organizational structures and cultures on policies and practices. In the United States, for example, most undergrad-uate admission decisions are conducted at the institutional level through a centralized admissions process. The evaluations of prospective students are completed by a professional staff focused solely on admissions. During the admissions process, United States institutions often consider not only the student's previous academic achievement but also other noncognitive fac-tors such as cocurricular involvements, family alumni status, gender, race, and socioeconomic status. Within many European countries, admissions decisions are generally conducted at the institutional level but through a decentralized process with the faculties and academic programs setting ad-mission criteria and making decisions. In these cases, the national ministry

NEW DIRECTIONS FOR HIGHER EDUCATION • DOI: 10.1002/he

or a centralized unit within the institution may facilitate the admission process through collection of such things as applications, data, and fees, but the evaluation of prospective students and their qualifications rests with the academic staff. Meanwhile, in many Asian countries, college admissions are controlled by the government through the national college entrance exam which results in students being assigned to a college or university based on their score in the exam. Here the national ministries assume the role of evaluator of prospective students, and previous academic achievement is usually the only factor considered in the college admission decisions. The differences in admission processes and their impacts on institutional policies and practices cannot be overstated. As such, a significant policy issue, such as student retention, in one country may be a nonissue in another country.

Moving Forward: Assessment, Evaluation, and Research

As assessment becomes part of the common terminology in international higher education, scholars and practitioners need to critically examine important questions regarding the future of assessment and evaluation in higher education. First, we need to ask ourselves why we conduct assessments. As discussed earlier in this chapter, assessment can be used to improve student learning or as an accountability measure. In today's higher education environment, practitioners may be required to conduct assessment for both purposes. However, these two purposes tend to conflict with each other in practice, and tools designed for the improvement purpose may not work well as an indicator of accountability and vice versa. For example, the NSSE was designed as an assessment tool to improve educational practices. Researchers have shown that student engagement has a wide range of variance within an institution (Kuh, 2003), which means at any higher education institution there are both highly engaged students and minimally engaged students. The purpose of NSSE is to help faculty and higher education practitioners identify improvement strategies within their institutions. Using NSSE for the purpose of international ranking of higher education institutions is inappropriate because aggregated institutional engagement indices do not present the full picture of student engagement at any campus and, indeed, not all the items on the assessment may apply to institutions outside of the United States. Therefore, higher education practitioners must have a clear vision on the purpose of their assessment and knowledge of the appropriate use of assessment tools.

Second, higher education practitioners must also consider whether to adopt, adapt, or devise alternative assessment or evaluation tools from other countries and cultures. Assessment tools are products of a particular social, educational, and cultural context as noted above in relation to NSSE. A good assessment tool in one setting can be totally inadequate in another setting. Researchers and practitioners may be tempted to adopt or translate established assessment tools from another country or language, but doing so requires intimate knowledge of the cultural differences between the assessment's developer and adopter. Two countries that speak the same language can have very different educational context. Thus, practitioners should not assume that an assessment that works for one English-speaking country will automatically maintain its validity and reliability when adopted into another English-speaking country. The same principle is also applicable to translated assessment tools—just because the survey or test is translated correctly does not guarantee it will maintain its validity and reliability when utilized in a different social and cultural context.

Third, higher education institutions should invest in personnel and facilities whose primary responsibility is to conduct and coordinate assessment and evaluation. As we mentioned earlier, most institutions in the United States now have an office of institutional research. However, the responsibilities of the IR offices vary from one institution to another and not all institutions have consolidated assessment and evaluation responsibilities into a centralized office. Establishing an office to take charge of assessment, evaluation, and institutional research requires financial, personnel, and physical resources and they do not come cheap. To establish an accountability culture as well as a culture of evidence-based improvement and good practice in assessment, higher education leaders must communicate to external stakeholders such as policy makers and business leaders the importance of assessment and evaluation in 21st-century higher education. Higher education leaders must also hire the right personnel to be in charge of assessment, evaluation, and institutional research. Good student affairs assessment and institutional-research practices need both technical and context knowledge. In short, people in charge of assessment and evaluation must have knowledge in statistics and measurement as well as cultural awareness and knowledge of the institutional and policy environment and the relationships between assessment, evaluation, and accreditation or quality assurance standards (Terenzini, 1993, 2013).

Finally, professional development is a must for assessment and evaluation professionals. Not only will they need to follow the development of assessment and evaluation tools such as new surveys and tests, but they also need to learn new statistical methods, assessment related technology, accreditation and quality assurance standards, and laws, policies, and rules that govern higher education. Additionally, today's assessment and evaluation professionals must develop cultural awareness and an understanding of the international educational context. We recommend practitioners join professional organizations such as AIR (www.airweb.org) or ENQA (www.enqa.eu), which are devoted to advancing assessment and evaluation in higher education, and regularly attend professional conferences and workshops. Practitioners should also pay attention to new developments in organizations such as the Centre for Global Higher Education at University College London, the Worldwide Universities Network, and Boston College's Center for International Higher Education that are conducting research on global higher education. Regular reading of higher education news nationally and internationally (such as universityworldnews.com) by devoting part of their work hours to keeping up-to-date is another good habit. Finally, in this age of social network and mobile technology, assessment, and evaluation professionals should utilize new technologies for networking, knowledge advancement, and professional development. Social network websites, which have dedicated sections devoted to professionals within academia such as LinkedIn.com, ResearchGate.net and Academia.edu, can help develop a knowledge network for assessment and evaluation professionals.

Conclusion

The history of accountability and assessment movement in the United States and other countries suggests that higher education institutions tend to be reactive instead of proactive when it comes to assessment and evaluation. Though formal and informal classroom assessment has existed since the dawn of organized education, systematic efforts to coordinate assessment and evaluation for institutional improvement only began when institutions were forced to do so by policy makers and accreditation or quality assurance officials. In this chapter, we briefly discussed the definition of assessment and evaluation in the higher education context, the different uses of assessment, the evolution of accountability, assessment, and institutional research in the United States and other countries, and good practices in adopting assessment and evaluation across borders and cultures. It is our wish that higher education scholars and practitioners take initiative to establish an assessment culture within their institutions and advance the scholarship of assessment and evaluation in a cross-border and cross-cultural manner. If student learning is what we care about, we should not be reactive but proactive in assessing and improving the conditions that foster student learning and development.

References

Adam, S. (2008). *Learning outcomes current development in Europe: Update on the issues and applications of learning outcomes associated with the Bologna Process* (The Scottish Government Report). Retrieved from http://www.aef-europe.be/documents /Edinburgh_2.pdf

Arminio, J., & Creamer, D. G. (2004, Spring). Promoting quality in higher education: The Council for the Advancement of Standards (CAS) celebrates 25 years. *Leadership Exchange*, 18–21.

Bennett, W. J., & Wilezol, D. (2013). *Is college worth it?: A former United States Secretary of Education and a liberal arts graduate expose the broken promise of higher education.* Nashville, TN: Thomas Nelson.

Chen, Y., & Hoshower, L. B. (2003). Student evaluation of teaching effectiveness: An assessment of student perception and motivation. *Assessment & Evaluation in Higher Education, 28,* 71–88.

Ewell, P. T. (2002). An emerging scholarship: A brief history of assessment. In T. W. Banta (Ed.), *Building a scholarship of assessment* (pp. 3–25). San Francisco, CA: Jossey-Bass.

Fuller, C. (2011). *The history and origins of survey items for the Integrated Postsecondary Education Data System (NPEC 2012-833)*. Retrieved from http://nces.ed.gov /pubs2012/2012833.pdf

Johnstone, D. B., Teixeira, P. N., Rosa, M. J., & Vossensteyn, H. (2008). Introduction. In P. N. Teixeira, D. B. Johnstone, M. J. Rosa, & H. Vossensteyn (Eds.), *Cost-sharing and accessibility in higher education: A fairer deal?* (pp. 1–18). Dordrecht, Netherland: Springer.

Kezar, A. (2009). Supporting and enhancing student learning through partnerships with academic colleagues. In G. S. McClellan & J. Stringer (Eds.), *The handbook of student affairs administration* (3rd ed., pp. 435–455). San Francisco, CA: Jossey-Bass.

Kuh, G. D. (2003). What we're learning about student engagement from NSSE: Benchmarks for effective educational practices. *Change: The Magazine of Higher Learning*, 35(2), 24–32. doi:10.1080/00091380309604090

Marginson, S. (2006). Dynamics of national and global competition. *Higher Education Forum*, 7, 1–9.

Mathies, C. (2015). Transnational IR collaborations. In K. Webber & A. Calderon (Eds.), *Institutional research and planning in higher education: Global contexts and themes* (pp. 28–39). New York, NY: Routledge.

Merriam-Webster. (2015). *Assessment*. Retrieved from www.merriam-webster.com /dictionary/assessment

Middaugh, M. F. (2010). *Planning and assessment in higher education: Demonstrating institutional effectiveness*. San Francisco, CA: Jossey-Bass.

Rhatigan, J. J. (2009). From the people up: A brief history of student affairs administration. In G. S. McClellan & J. Stringer (Eds.), *The handbook of student affairs administration* (3rd ed., pp. 1–20). San Francisco, CA: Jossey-Bass.

Richard, D. J. (2012). The history of institutional research. In R. D. Howard, G. W. McLaughlin, & W. E. Knight (Eds.), *The handbook of institutional research* (pp. 3–21). San Francisco, CA: Jossey-Bass.

Suskie, L. (2004). *Assessing student learning: A common sense guide*. San Francisco, CA: Anker.

Terenzini, P. T. (1993). On the nature of institutional research and the knowledge and skills it requires. *Research in Higher Education*, 34(1), 1–10.

Terenzini, P. T. (2013). "On the nature of institutional research" revisited: Plus ça change...? *Research in Higher Education*, 54(2), 137–148.

Thelin, J. R. (2011). *A history of American higher education* (2nd ed.). Baltimore, MD: John Hopkins University Press.

Upcraft, M. L., & Schuh, J. H. (1996). *Assessment in student affairs: A guide for practitioners*. San Francisco, CA: Jossey-Bass.

U.S. Department of Education (2015). *IPEDS survey components and data collection cycle*. Washington, DC: Author. Retrieved from https://nces.ed.gov/ipeds/resource/survey_ components.asp#surveycomponents

U.S. Department of Health and Human Services, Centers for Disease Control and Prevention, Office of the Director, Office of Strategy and Innovation. (2011). *Introduction to program evaluation for public health programs: A self-study guide*. Atlanta, GA: Centers for Disease Control and Prevention. Retrieved from http://www .cdc.gov/eval/guide/cover/index.htm

P. DANIEL CHEN is an associate professor in the Department of Counseling and Higher Education at the University of North Texas in the United States.

CHARLES MATHIES is a senior expert in the Division of Strategic Planning and Development at the University of Jyväskylä in Finland.

10

This chapter explores institutional capacity building in cross-border student affairs and services. The focus is on human capital and its importance to international higher education within local contexts.

Staffing for Success

Brett Perozzi, Tricia Seifert, Mary Ann Bodine Al-Sharif

As enumerated throughout this volume, the substantial increase in cross-border education over the past 15 years (Knight & Morshidi, 2011) has had a tremendous impact on educational delivery and student learning and development. The need to help students navigate the multifaceted landscape of a globalized tertiary education system and also obtain the requisite skills and abilities to be competitive in an increasingly international workplace necessitates that faculty and staff approach their work broadly, conceptualizing their roles as educators within a cross-border context while understanding their local environment.

The authors draw from a recent international research study (Seifert, Perozzi, Bodine Al-Sharif, Li, & Wildman, 2014) to discuss the state of student affairs and services internationally in terms of educational pathways and professional development. The authors discuss cross-border capacity building where staff members working outside their home context contribute to developing capacity while also increasing their own understanding of student affairs and services and tertiary education internationally. To this end, staff members who have worked abroad may contribute their learning from international contexts to better support both domestic students and those studying outside their home jurisdictions, and staff who remain in their home jurisdictions can educate themselves to better understand international dynamics and contexts.

Intercultural Competence

In a cross-border educational paradigm, it is increasingly important for faculty and staff to orient their work and self-understanding of their roles to be that of *educators*. This cross-border paradigm recognizes the significant increase in student, faculty, and staff mobility, and the potential interdependence among tertiary education and employment systems. Attracting, hiring, and retaining staff who see themselves as educators, and who possess a comprehensive understanding of cross-cultural competence, can be

New Directions for Higher Education, no. 175, Fall 2016 © 2016 Wiley Periodicals, Inc.
Published online in Wiley Online Library (wileyonlinelibrary.com) • DOI: 10.1002/he.20203

critical to the longevity of higher education organizations. Not only do staff need to understand what it means to live and work in another cultural context, those in their native countries must also understand the meaning of cross-cultural competence as it relates to student development and success (Bresciani, 2008; West, 2012).

Competence related to internationalization has many forms and names, such as cultural competence and intercultural competence. In keeping with definitions from Chapter 1 of this volume, Reimers (2010) asserts that competencies include "the attitudinal and ethical dispositions that make it possible to interact peacefully, respectfully and productively with fellow human beings from diverse geographies" (p. 184). Deardorff (2006) highlights three common elements in definitions of intercultural competence as "awareness, valuing, and understanding of cultural differences; experiencing other cultures; and self-awareness of one's own culture" (p. 247). Gudykunst (1991, in Pusch 2009) wisely suggests the following intercultural skills: mindfulness, cognitive flexibility, tolerance for ambiguity, behavioral flexibility, and cross-cultural empathy.

Although the range of international skills, knowledge, and abilities is broad, similarities in both approach and specific competencies do exist. Several international organizations have made great strides in providing guidance in the approach to international competence in serving students through various modalities within student affairs and services. For example, in the United States, ACPA—College Student Educators International and NASPA—Student Affairs Administrators in Higher Education (2015) released an updated statement on professional competencies for student affairs practitioners in which cultural competence, inclusive practice, and nationality as a salient component of identity, are discussed in terms of multiple competencies. Although competencies will vary by culture, locality, and philosophies of practice, it is important to identify broad competencies and instill in staff the ability to distill and/or adapt these concepts in a local community to produce the best results for students. It is critical not to impose a singular lens, particularly a Western one, when approaching cross-border higher education and student affairs and services.

Not only do staff, faculty, and students need to understand what it means to live and work in another cultural context, student affairs and services practitioners in their native countries must also understand the meaning of cross-cultural competence as it relates to student development and success. Laying the foundation with clearly articulated competencies will help organizations build capacity by developing staff who have the knowledge and skills to best support students in their success.

Building Capacity

The fact that essential competencies will vary from a cross-border perspective necessitates that capacity building be unique to each country or region.

Myriad factors impact the ability to build capacity, with core competencies being just one among others such as the status or acceptance of student affairs and services in the academy, resource availability and allocation, government policy, and much more.

Approaches to the work of student affairs and services vary significantly around the world (Ludeman, Osfield, Hidalgo, Oste, & Wang, 2009). These approaches may be influenced by the guiding ideologies of education, the degree to which students are seen as adults, and the perception of the role student affairs and services staff members play in the tertiary environment.

In most parts of the world, practitioners come to student affairs and services work from various educational and career backgrounds (Seifert et al., 2014) that shape their professional orientations. This variation in disciplinary background is likely to result in higher levels of collective competence within teams and among working groups, yet with a lower level of common understanding and approach. As da Costa (2006, in Bresciani, 2008) brilliantly summarizes, "the social learning process of a collective is to acquire new personnel who bring with them knowledge and sets of expectations that differ substantially from those already held by the collective" (p. 3). Although identifying common ground among a collective of staff members from diverse backgrounds takes time, a primary motivation for individuals doing student affairs and services work is having a direct impact on students (Seifert et al., 2014), an aim characteristic of any educator. Building from this common motivation, institutional leaders can call on the diversity of skills and knowledge bases associated with various educational pathways to develop staff members' international competence.

Building capacity means that student affairs and services staff must not only become culturally competent, but also teach and serve as ambassadors so that others may begin to understand cultural differences and develop their cultural competence. Understanding the big picture of cross-border education while developing a cogent philosophy of organizational development will assist educational leaders in building capacity for their organizations, and sustaining it over time. Recognizing the educational and career backgrounds of staff, combined with an understanding of international competence, a commitment to hiring and training competent staff, and recognizing and overcoming organizational inertia to identify and measure success will help build capacity for higher education institutions.

Interacting with colleagues from a host of tertiary educational contexts can enhance staff members' capacity for intercultural competence. Expatriate workers, those who work in a context outside their passport country, may be instrumental in fostering such interactions. These workers can provide ideas and promising practices in developing the institution's perspective with regard to its student affairs and services offerings. A key element is for those originating from a Western perspective to be cognizant of cultural nuance and mores, and keep context in mind for programs and services that make sense for that particular institution (Roberts, 2015).

NEW DIRECTIONS FOR HIGHER EDUCATION • DOI: 10.1002/he

Diversifying the Workforce

Although recruiting and hiring a diversified staff is not a simple task, technological advancements and the increased mobility of individuals and industry (Vance & Paik, 2015) have resulted in a more expansive employment pool. Whether working abroad or stationed domestically, staff are in a worldwide market. As long as they have the knowledge base and skills, internationally competent staff members provide the greatest sustainable competitive advantage for an organization.

For expatriates, there can be variances in exposure to the host culture (Haslberger, Brewster, & Hippler, 2014). Some expatriates live in domesticated environmental bubbles through expatriate compounds, and others are absorbed into the host environment living among the local community. Either example requires cross-cultural competency at varying levels of comparative norms, economics, social and family relationships, governmental systems, and working environments. Roberts (2015) notes that due to the adoption and adaptation of Western higher educational practices in emerging international higher education centers, educators in the West are often tapped for their expertise in developing educational initiatives. However, notable attention and caution must be given in this process to grow authentic, local educational endeavors as opposed to replicated Western ideologies and interpretations of higher education. By contextualizing educational programs and services to the needs of the host nations, expatriates working abroad provide cross-border competencies for these educational environments.

With increased numbers of international students studying abroad each year (IIE, 2015) and providing economic and social benefits to their hosting nations (IIE, 2012), the importance of a domestic internationally competent staff increases. Likewise, hiring internationally competent staff can support retention and help create a context in which students can learn and thrive. Training and a focus on international issues and problems also provides a common knowledge base across the organization. Because each context will be unique, this can reinforce a sense of belonging and community within a diverse student body. Understanding the uniqueness of place and the ability of staff to function within various cultural contexts is critical for international student affairs and services.

Cultural Variation and Common Understanding

The desire to assist students with their learning and collegiate experience and to support the systems that facilitate these programs and services is a common element among most countries. To provide services that support student needs, understanding the local and regional context is critical. The vision of serving students must meet cultural expectations, which can lead to a dichotomy of values in cross-border efforts and multi-campus institutions specifically (Roberts, 2015). Where student affairs and services is not an established profession, this dichotomy and potential for misunderstanding can be further exacerbated.

In some Chinese institutions, staff members work directly with students in areas such as accommodation and international student services, yet top leaders are experienced faculty members appointed to their roles. For example, student mentors in China (called *Banganbu*), provide core student support functions for as many as 50 undergraduates and are entrusted with significant responsibility for the success and well-being of these students (Xiao, 2013). The cultural context is critical and adopting or adapting a Western paradigm could lead to misunderstanding.

Although most faculty pursue a specific discipline and subsequently teach and research in that area, student affairs and services staff often cross over from academic fields or other jobs and careers entirely, prior to working in higher education (Seifert et al., 2014). They have experienced a wide range of training and development approaches, and have often worked in organizational cultures other than higher education.

Similar to educational variation, great opportunity exists to learn about, honor, and highlight the various skills and competencies staff bring to the collective organization. For example, in Seifert et al. (2014), the majority of respondents from Africa hold degrees in nursing-related disciplines. In this case, student health and well-being needs may influence the educational background of those providing student affairs and services.

With each discipline having its own subculture, it can be challenging to bridge these ideologies, while exposing staff to various ideas and ways for approaching the work. Creating a common philosophy around the approach to student affairs and services work is essential at the institutional level, however, it takes on an entirely different perspective when viewed by country, region, or internationally. The concept is not easy to aggregate, and there are those who would argue it should not be. While globalization tends to propel nations and worldwide efforts, it brings together ideology for increased understanding, whereas, the internationalization movement carves out individualized spaces in which various forms of student affairs and services can thrive.

In Europe, the Bologna Process brought together several countries in an effort to establish degrees that are comparable across international borders, a more solidified and organized method of acknowledging the transferring of credits, educational mobility across borders, and a higher quality educational experience (Gaston, 2010). However, as discussed in Chapter 2, the Bologna Process accomplished much more than this in that it forced governmental systems of Europe to rethink educational standards, workforce certifications, and economic disparities. It also revealed mounting tensions within higher-education institutions that were competing for available resources, specifically the acquisition of talent among faculty, staff, and students, and the desire to achieve high institutional rankings (Kehm,

NEW DIRECTIONS FOR HIGHER EDUCATION • DOI: 10.1002/he

2010). This example furthers the understanding and potential dichotomy surrounding globalization while maintaining individual characteristics and unique aspects of cultural variation.

Professional Preparation and Development

Professional preparation, defined as formal learning characterized by credentials, and professional development, defined as ongoing informal learning, may be considered as two sides of the same coin (Seifert, Perozzi, & Li, in press). Depending on the person, staff members may seek opportunities to strengthen their international competence and career skills either through formal educational coursework and credential pathways or informally through self-directed learning.

Where postgraduate programs are available in higher education/ student affairs (primarily in the United States), students can study this area as a discrete field for which a cannon of literature exists and curriculum is well established. In developing one's international competence, it is imperative to recognize the norms, values, and assumptions advanced within the United States paradigm of student affairs practice and professional preparation. Faculty and students in these graduate programs can develop competence and prepare themselves in three primary ways to become internationalists.

- Faculty teaching in professional preparation programs may infuse international concepts throughout the curriculum and create an environment for cross-border learning (Des Chenes, Ellis, & Reeve, 2013).
- Faculty may teach specialized courses that help students better understand the myriad of approaches to international student affairs and services.
- Graduate students can interact directly with the variety of internationalization programs embedded on campus.

Practically, a graduate credential in this area can be helpful for career advancement, but for those striving to work in cross-border environments, gaining skills and experiences to develop their intercultural competence is essential (Deardorff, 2006).

Opportunity for professional development varies tremendously worldwide. Professional associations in countries and regions where they exist play a key role in developing such opportunities. Programs offering short-term engagement through exchanges and longer-term experiences such as internships or job shadowing are growing in number and are a wonderful way to enhance one's international knowledge. Professional associations also offer training programs, conferences, webinars, publications, and other educational programming—all forms of informal learning that can meet the

NEW DIRECTIONS FOR HIGHER EDUCATION • DOI: 10.1002/he

international competency development needs of student affairs and services staff (Seifert et al., 2014). In addition to learning, there is a clear need to support research from a cross-border perspective in which staff work together to publish and present data, ideas, and promising practices.

Many opportunities exist for staff to become engaged across borders and to learn about international student affairs and services. For example, in many African countries, professional development is frequently sponsored by universities, on topics of interest to student affairs and services administrators, such as finance, management, and leadership (E. Kyagaba. Personal Communication, February 22, 2012). By supporting sabbatical leaves and short- or long-term study tours, institutions can build organizational capacity by assisting faculty and staff in gaining in-depth international experience. For example, in Saudi Arabia, the King Abdullah University of Science and Technology (KAUST) is purposefully designed to provide opportunities for native faculty and staff to partner with international colleagues in researching problems of local, regional, and global significance (KAUST, 2015). Not only does this aid in developing a knowledge-based economy, it also provides opportunity for native faculty and staff to engage in international professional development within the research arena. To date, KAUST through cross-border collaboration, development, and research has published more than 4,000 publications with 35% appearing in the top 10 research journals.

Ping (1999) suggests that staff have direct experiences with other cultures, and that they must have " ... an interest in the world and its diverse peoples, in geography, in global history, and in the contemporary political and economic realities of various regions in the world" (pp. 20–21). Using Perozzi and Ramos' (2016) list of potential staff development opportunities as a starting point, the authors offer the following approaches that enhance international and cross-border understanding and competence:

- Engage international colleagues in research and writing projects.
- Participate in formal exchange programs offered by a host of organizations.
- Interact with those doing international work and remain current on international issues.
- Explore another language.
- Seek to host international faculty and staff.
- Establish international current events conversations.
- Offer personalized discussion opportunities for international students.
- Develop programs that include an international perspective.
- Engage international students in program development, and invite them to take on leadership positions.
- Start or support international clubs and student organizations.

NEW DIRECTIONS FOR HIGHER EDUCATION • DOI: 10.1002/he

- Provide opportunities for synchronous distance learning and/or seminars in partnership with affiliated institutions abroad.
- Provide opportunities for intercultural dialogue.
- Partner with affiliated institutions abroad for research and exchange opportunities.

Conclusions and Implications

Building organizational capacity for cross-border higher education is a critical need. More specific to personnel, institutions must cultivate internationally competent staff by clearly defining for the organization what internationalization entails, what essential elements it includes, and then train staff appropriately while measuring the extent of the collective success. Embedding the values of culturally specific ideologies within the broader international context and making them overt will help organizations understand the importance of cultural competence, which fosters an environment in which students can obtain the requisite skills and abilities to compete in an international workplace.

Given the various conceptualizations of student affairs and services, it remains essential that biases be checked and paradigms acknowledged. Being successful in cross-border higher education requires that organizations and individuals recognize cultural nuance, their own positionalities, and build into the student affairs and services culture the ability to adapt and continually learn. Attaining cultural competence is a lifetime activity and cannot be achieved in the short term; however, the foundation can be laid and the path to success should be marked by appropriate milestones along the way.

References

ACPA–College Student Educators International and NASPA–Student Affairs Administrators in Higher Education (2015). *Professional competency areas for student affairs educators*. Retrieved from http://www.naspa.org/images/uploads/main/ACPA_NASPA _Professional_Competencies_FINAL.pdf.

Bresciani, M. L. (2008). Global competencies in student affairs/services professionals: A literature synthesis. *College Student Journal, 42*, 906–919.

Deardorff, D. (2006). Identification and assessment of intercultural competence as a student outcome of internationalization. *Journal of Studies in International Education, 10*, 241–266.

Des Chenes, O., Ellis, S., & Reeve, A. (2013). *Global competence: The importance of international: Experiences for student affairs graduate preparatory programs and professionals.* NASPA Knowledge Communities. Excellence in Practice. Washington, DC: NASPA.

Gaston, P. L (2010). *The challenge of Bologna: What United States higher education has to learn from Europe, and why it matters that we learn it.* Sterling, VA: Stylus.

Haslberger, A., Brewster, C., & Hippler, T. (2014). *Managing performance abroad: A new model for understanding expatriate adjustment.* New York, NY: Routledge.

Institute of International Education. (2012, November 12). *Open Doors 2012: International student enrollment increased by 6 percent.* Open Doors Report on International Educational Exchange. Retrieved from http://www.iie.org/Who-We-Are/News-and-Events/Press-Center/Press-Releases/2012/2012-11-13-Open-Doors-International-Students.

Institute of International Education. (2015). Open Doors 2014 "Fast Facts." Retrieved from http://www.iie.org/Who-We-Are/News-and-Events/Press-Center/Press-Releases/2015/2015-11-16-Open-Doors-Data.

KAUST. (2015, February 24). *From startup to maturity: Leadership and role of a new university.* Retrieved from http://www.kaust.edu.sa/times-higher-education-mena-universities-summit.html

Kehm, B. M. (2010). Quality in European higher education: The influence of the Bologna Process. *Change: The Magazine of Higher Learning, 42*(3), 40–46.

Knight, J., & Morshidi, S. (2011). The complexities and challenges of regional education hubs: Focus on Malaysia. *Higher Education, 62,* 593–606.

Ludeman, R., Osfield, K., Hidalgo, E., Oste, D., & Wang, H. (2009). *Student affairs and services in higher education: Global foundations, issues and best practices.* Paris, France: UNESCO.

Perozzi, B., & Ramos, E. R. (2016). Student affairs and services in global perspective. In G. McClellend, & J. Stringer (Eds.), *Handbook of student affairs administration* (4th ed.). San Francisco, CA: Jossey Bass.

Ping, C. J. (1999). An expanded international role for student affairs. In J. Dalton (Ed.), *International developments changing student affairs practice* (New Directions for Student Services 86, pp. 13–21). San Francisco, CA: Jossey-Bass.

Pusch, M. D. (2009). The interculturally competent global leader. In D. Deardorff (Ed.), *The SAGE handbook of intercultural competence* (pp. 66–84). Thousand Oaks, CA: SAGE.

Reimers, F. (2010). Educating for global competence. In J. E. Cohen, & M. B. Malin (Eds.), *International perspectives on the goals of universal basic and secondary education* (pp. 183–202). New York, NY: Routledge.

Roberts, D. C. (2015). International perspectives: Expatriate workers in international higher education. *Journal of College & Character, 16*(1), 37–43.

Seifert, T., Perozzi, B., Bodine Al-Sharif, M. A., Li, W., & Wildman, K. (2014). *Student affairs & services in global perspective: A preliminary exploration of practitioners' background, roles and professional development.* Toronto, Canada: IASAS.

Seifert, T., Perozzi, B., & Li, W. (in press). Two sides of the coin: Educational pathways and professional learning. In K. Osfield, B. Perozzi, L. Bardill Moscaritolo, & R. Shea (Eds.), *Internationalizing student affairs and services: Providing support to students globally in higher education.* Washington, DC: NASPA.

Vance, C. M., & Paik, Y (2015). *Managing a global workforce: Challenges and opportunities in international human resource management* (3rd ed.). New York, NY: Routledge.

West, C. (2012). *Toward globally competent pedagogy.* Washington, DC: NAFSA: Association of International Educators.

Xiao, M. (2013). *A comparative study: Student affairs in Chinese and American higher education.* Unpublished Master's Thesis. University of Denver.

BRETT PEROZZI is associate vice president for student affairs at Weber State University. He is the immediate past chair of NASPA's Global Advisory Board, and has published numerous book chapters and journal articles on international student affairs and services.

TRICIA SEIFERT is an associate professor and program leader in the Adult & Higher Education program at Montana State University and maintains a faculty appointment at the Ontario Institute for Studies in Education at the University of Toronto. She examines how organizational structure and culture influence student success, the multiple dimensions of student learning and success, and the role of student affairs and services in fostering success internationally.

MARY ANN BODINE AL-SHARIF is a doctoral candidate at the University of Oklahoma and serves as the Director of Recruitment and Admissions at Oklahoma City Community College. Her current research interests include exploring the lives of students who define themselves as living between worlds within global movements of educational reform.

NEW DIRECTIONS FOR HIGHER EDUCATION • DOI: 10.1002/he

11

Following chapters that have offered examples and tools relevant to higher education institutions that wish to enhance student learning and development, this chapter summarizes and extends the conversation of how true partnerships in international higher education can be cultivated to achieve the deepest impact.

Innovation Partnerships to Enhance Student Learning and Development

Dennis C. Roberts, Susan R. Komives

Educators are growing in their understanding of the power of the student experience in international settings; however, sharing across institutions and countries is a challenge that requires very different approaches to student learning and development. With due caution about transferring educational practices that might be inappropriate, this book shared examples and advocated theories and models that can be used by educators, policy makers and funders of cross-border, and international higher education. The following are points of consensus around what is most important in student learning and development.

Student Learning and Development as a Focus

Enhancing student learning and development not only serves students more fully, resulting in greater satisfaction, retention, and success but more importantly in our view, it has the potential to transform students' understanding of their world and help them become more effective as they engage it. This is not to say that service, good administration, and management are unimportant. The positive impact of student affairs in the United States during the 20th century was at least equally focused on enhancing the quality of student learning and development as it was easing administrative processes and making university education convenient or consumer focused.

Motivations Matter. The "heuristics of diffusion" described in Chapter 2 proposed five reasons why educators and institutions modify their practices. Discerning the motivation for enhancing student learning

NEW DIRECTIONS FOR HIGHER EDUCATION, no. 175, Fall 2016 © 2016 Wiley Periodicals, Inc.
Published online in Wiley Online Library (wileyonlinelibrary.com) • DOI: 10.1002/he.20204

and development is particularly key, especially when many institutions may have multiple or overlapping motivations.

The formation of student government, a practice that is typical in most universities in the United States, may serve well as an example of the different motivations of educators or institutions as they transfer, adapt, hedge, or avoid this approach in cross-border settings. A "learning" motivation could result from international educators reading about the benefit of providing students a voice in institutional policies and programs that affect their lives. "Imitative" (or "mimetic") motivation would result from imitating institutions that are renowned for the practice; for example, Thomas Jefferson's advocacy for student participation at the University of Virginia during its founding in the 19th century established a precedent that has impacted many institutions in the United States and elsewhere. A "normative" example of student involvement can be found in the prevalence of student participation through the *Studentenwerks* of many German universities. "Competition" was at least a partial motivation for the Universidad de Monterrey example provided in Chapter 6. This leadership model not only enhanced learning and development related to community and civic participation, it distinguished Universidad de Monterrey as it competes with peer institutions. Finally, coercion could be the driving motivation for cases in which students demand a voice in governance or where the country in which an institution functions requires such a mechanism to respond to students' consumer concerns.

An institution's motivation for considering how a student government should be formulated would also impact who the major stakeholders would be as the early work of establishing the student government is undertaken. If the motivation were based on learning from best practice or imitating exemplary institutions, faculty in social science disciplines might be some of the best allies. By contrast, if institutional competition is the primary motivation, those involved in administration (especially student recruitment) as well as managers who are concerned with fiscal and organizational welfare may offer the most significant support.

Transfer, Adapt, Hedge, or Avoid?   Continuing with the example of formulating a student government, the process of design should reflect the unique conditions in the settings. Transferring the idea of student government with essentially the same approach used in the United States would most likely occur in cases in which the focus is on learning from best practices among similar institutions with comparable student populations. However, imitating exemplary universities should be adapted for a setting in which student involvement has not been a long tradition and custom. In this case, imitation might at least start by limiting the degree to which students were allowed to offer input on policy and program decisions. The practice of formulating student government may even be hedged or avoided all together in a country that did not have democratic rule. Hedging could be accomplished by seeking the sanction of those who could perceive the empowerment of student participation as a threat to political stability. Student governance should perhaps be postponed or avoided when no supportive authority can be secured.

This analysis of the motivations for transferring, adapting, hedging, or avoiding student-government models assumed that student governance was consistent across universities in the United States; this assumption is, in fact, not true. Even in a national context in which student government is a routine or normative approach, the degree to which students have substantive input on institutional decisions varies based on institution type, nature of its students, and the college or university's philosophy of learning. Cross-border environments require careful and critical examination of the motivations for considering a practice, the degree of cultural distance, and the institutional supports required to be successful. Choosing to adapt, hedge, or avoid, rather than simply transferring a practice, may be more defensible approaches given the combination of these factors.

Special Considerations.   In addition to the idea of student governance, there are a number of student learning and development practices that are likely to vary based on the cultural composition of students and the national or regional context of the college or university. Career decision making, perceptions of counseling/psychological services, and collaboration among faculty and staff offer good illustrations of this point.

Career Decision Making.   Drawing from Denny's experience working with Qatar Foundation's Education City and from the results of the Qatar Study Tour and Young Professionals Institute in 2010 described in the editors' notes, the idea of career decision making, vocational calling, and motivation for work can be very different when working with students of different cultural backgrounds. Kagitcibasi (2005) proposed that students are very different in relation to agency (degree of functional independence) and interpersonal distance (the degree of emotional/practical connection to others), and Dwairy, Achoui, Abouserie, and Farah (2006) studied connectedness specifically among Arab families. Taken together, these analyses confirmed the experience of working with students from approximately 100 countries, largely collectivist cultures from throughout northern Africa, the Middle East, and Asia. Career decision making for these students balanced student independent decision making with deference to family, which contrasts with the prevalent Western practice of relying on student autonomous decision making. In reality, students' majors and career decisions were often tipped more in the direction of family. The decision about academic major and eventual work was significantly influenced by the degree to which it brought honor and prestige to nuclear and extended family, was perceived positively by community associates, and in some cases was viewed as a patriotic duty to government and national leaders that students held in high esteem.

Counseling.   Willingness to seek help through counseling and psychological services varies among all student groups but is likely to represent even greater variation in cross-border environments. Related to the previous description of career decision making, students may rely on parents, family, and community associates for support rather than pursue professional counseling support. In addition, the mere availability of counseling and psychological services may have resulted in students not having had much exposure to these services as a natural part of life experience. There are even circumstances under which students may not feel protected in terms of confidentiality should they seek counseling assistance. All these factors contribute to the possibility that students from broad cultural/national backgrounds may not seek help in the same ways as students do in Western contexts. Chapter 6 addressed, in very interesting ways, how the protections and encouragement of students from Chinese one-child families may result in vulnerabilities under challenging circumstances. Particularly under these conditions, helping students understand that seeking help is not a sign of weakness but can contribute to their efficacy and resilience is very important, and the approach will likely be different from conventional counseling practices in the United States.

Faculty and Staff Collaboration. The final example of cultural/contextual variation, collaboration among faculty and staff, is heavily influenced by the findings reported in Chapter 10. Educators who work in cross-border settings are more diverse than those found in the typical university in the United States. In some cases, this results in faculty serving in important leadership roles in newly formed student affairs departments. The very positive outcome of this is that faculty disciplinary expertise can find its way into student affairs approaches as well as the fact that the dichotomies found in some United States universities between faculty and staff are absent, resulting in enhanced opportunities to cooperate and support one another's work. Some of the international higher-education settings are emerging in ways that foster broad institutional commitment to student learning and development goals such as we found in the Chapter 8 example of Singapore.

Cautions. These three examples reflect practices that are sometimes perceived to be normative but actually are not normative at all, requiring modification to the cross-border environment. There are also some practices that may be particularly sensitive across borders, justifying consideration if the practice should be considered at all. Intercollegiate sports and athletics in the United States began in ways consonant with what we currently consider to be club sports, intramural competitions, or recreation. Over time these have evolved in some United States universities to levels resembling major business enterprises with major budgets, salaries, and the complications that may come with this expanded scale. Cross-border higher education should carefully consider if the way big-time intercollegiate athletics now dominates some universities is in the best interest of new and developing institutions around the world. Political, religious, and social groups may also represent significant risks in some regions of the world. The phenomenon of Greek-letter organizations (fraternities and sororities) may look attractive to some undergraduate students in cross-border settings, but the potential misalignment of values of these groups may cause thoughtful educators to be ambivalent about them. Traditions are another aspect of campus culture that may be celebrated in the United States but sometimes have significant negative implications in cross-border education. Examples include where campus traditions, such as a spring fest or founder's day, go awry or where a risky competition is part of the ritual.

With each of the aforementioned examples of practices that can enhance student learning and development, it is important to recognize that some of the things that are most worth doing are also the most challenging. As Chapter 3 candidly revealed and our experience confirms, initiatives can be subject to a variety of situational or political influences that are out of our control. This may mean that timing or context will result in our not achieving our goals in some initiatives. Accepting this and continuing to work for positive change is essential if progress is to be made.

Growing Cross-Border Momentum

The focus on international and cross-border higher education is gathering momentum. The intent of this book is to support this growing movement and to urge those involved to carefully consider how to ensure that students' learning and development is a primary focus and beneficiary of these initiatives. Returning to the definitions we proposed in Chapter 1, we believe that many colleges and universities will be most comfortable pursuing internationalization rather than globalization. Internationalization has greater potential to preserve the character of the people, the values of the institutions, and to advance the purposes of the diverse array of institutions that now serve the growing world-wide student population. This internationalization can be implemented inside an institution without appreciable involvement of others outside the physical or intellectual boundaries of the college or university. However, some of the most powerful forms of internationalization are made possible through cross-border partnerships of various types.

There is growing advocacy for internationalization to be a responsibility that all higher education institutions should address. The International Association of Universities (IAU, 2016), with over 600 institutional members from throughout the world, has initiated important surveys, and offers policy statements and advisory services to assist their constituents with their internationalization projects. The American Council on Education (ACE, 2015) has been one of the most active proponents of internationalization among institutions in the United States. *International Higher Education Partnerships: A Global Review of Standards and Practices* (ACE, 2015) is consistent with the recommendations of this book, plus, it urges colleges and universities to pursue a comprehensive approach to internationalization

NEW DIRECTIONS FOR HIGHER EDUCATION • DOI: 10.1002/he

that connects, relates, and synchronizes resources and programs, including those that can be offered through the cocurriclum (Ward, 2016). Complementing the perspectives of the IAU and the ACE, this book focused on the student experience as an outcome of university internationalization efforts and encouraged those efforts designed to help students develop a "global self" (Killick, 2015), resulting from experiential learning that is intentional, specific, and related to each student's own sense of self.

Colleges and universities will enhance their impact and effectiveness if they establish authentic partnerships. Whether internal or external to the institution, it is critical to approach partnerships in ways that ensure mutual benefit. Adhering to the following principles will foster both authenticity and mutuality as internationalization initiatives are planned and implemented (Gore, 2012):

- Cultivate shared purpose and community among partners.
- Preserve brand identification and protect the reputation of all.
- Maintain an awareness and prioritization of multiple stakeholders.
- Align internal stakeholders with common values and aims.
- Articulate strong transparent corporate values.
- Develop awareness and sensitivity to cultural differences.
- Integrate description, analysis and the acquisition of lessons learned into the planning processes.
- Affirm divergent approaches.
- Maintain core competencies and sources of sustainable strategic advantage.

To these we would add (Roberts, 2015):

- Embrace disruptive and rapid change.
- Demonstrate stewardship of resources.
- Offer choices, not prescriptions.

The process of seeking mutual benefit becomes especially key and volatile when the rules of cultural interaction are different among partners. The GLOBE project (Brodbeck & Eisenbeiss, 2014; Kumar & Chhokar 2012) advocated that explicit attention be focused on the fit between key cultural variables and the leadership that would likely be effective in differing contexts when pursuing partnerships across borders. The Molinsky (2013) model can be used to think about the process of cross-border negotiation required when considering an international partnership. Molinsky advocates taking careful account of one's own cultural inclinations, analyzing the unique cultural expectations of the host setting, determining how one's own cultural inclination can be moderated to be more effective in embracing others, and finally thinking and acting in ways that are authentic while adapting to the other culture. All this is likely undertaken with the guidance of a helpful cultural advisor who can assist you in understanding and seeking more effective interaction.

Applying the Molinsky (2013) model to hypothetical negotiations between a university in the United States and a Middle East policy maker, it is likely that United States educators would be relatively direct, would project considerable enthusiasm for the prospects of partnering, would rely on spontaneous networking to access decision makers, would have no problem asserting their proposal, would promote themselves and their institution's merits without reservation, and all this would be done in highly transparent ways. By contrast, the potential Middle East policy maker would be more likely to be circumspect in relation to the prospective partnership, would be difficult to read in relation to enthusiasm about a proposal, would expect to be contacted through recognized authorities or brokered relationships, would be passive in the encounter (unlikely to ever say "no" but reluctant to offer "yes" as well), would not be inclined to assert superiority, and all this within a cautious and indirect communication style.

The cultural styles just mentioned are deliberately exaggerated, but from personal experience and observation of others' negotiations, these cultural encounters are frequently more, rather than less, complicated than this brief description. The only way to increase the possibility of positive outcomes is by cultivating a level of openness and willingness to reflect on one's own and the other culture in order to demonstrate responsiveness while still seeking to establish a "deal" in the partnership. Under these circumstances, it is particularly important to address the core values that are driving the change with specific attention to sustaining momentum in the face of potential resistance and reticence.

Conclusion

This volume was designed to communicate to a wide audience of educators throughout the world who seek to more fully understand the promise of quality higher education. Quality international higher education in the 21st century will increasingly depend on cross-border partnerships that are conceived and pursued with mutual respect and benefit at their core. Enhanced student learning and development can be more effectively achieved by considering what we know from student development and campus environment research and then applying a lens of culture and local/regional context to assure its relevance.

We propose that the cross-border higher education practices that are most likely to positively enhance student learning and development begin with knowing the need you seek to fulfill, then analyzing the conditions or problems you want to address, and finally engaging with others in curious and exploratory ways to improve the likelihood for success of your efforts. These basic principles must be undertaken with insightful and deft cultural understanding and dexterity.

References

American Council on Education. (2015). *International higher education partnerships: A global review of standards and practices.* Retrieved from www.acenet.edu/news-room /Documents/CIGE-Insights-Intl-Higher-Ed-Parternships.pdf

Brodbeck, F. C., & Eisenbeiss, S. (2014). Cross-cultural and global leadership. *Oxford Handbooks Online.* Oxford University Press. DOI: 10.1093/oxfordhb/9780199755615.013.032

Dwairy, M., Achoui, M., Abouserie, R., & Farah, A. (2006). Adolescent-family connectedness among Arabs. *Journal of Cross-Cultural Psychology, 37*(3), 248–261.

Gore, T. (2012). *Higher education across borders: Models of engagement and lessons from corporate strategy.* London, UK: The Observatory on Borderless Higher Education.

International Association of Universities. (2016). *Internationalization of higher education virtual resource center.* Retrieved from http://www.iau-aiu.net/content /internationalization

Kagitcibasi, C. (2005). Autonomy and relatedness in cultural context. *Journal of Cross-Cultural Psychology, 36,* 403–422.

Killick, D. (2015). *Developing the global student: Higher education in an era of globalization.* New York, NY: Routledge.

Kumar, R., & Chhokar, J. S. (2012). Cross-cultural leadership. *Oxford Handbooks Online.* Oxford University Press. DOI: 10.1093/oxfordhb/9780195398793.013.0014

Molinsky, A. (2013). *Global dexterity: How to adapt your behavior across cultures without losing yourself in the process.* Cambridge, MA: Harvard Business Review Press.

Roberts, D. C. (2015). Internationalizing higher education and student affairs. *About Campus: Enriching the Student Learning Experience, 20*(2), 8–15.

Ward, H. (2016). Internationalizing the cocurriculum: a three-part series, Internationalization and Student Affairs. Retrieved from https://www.acenet.edu/news-room/Pages /Internationalization-in-Action.aspx

DENNIS C. ROBERTS *was associate provost of Hamad bin Khalifa University and assistant vice president for education with the Qatar Foundation from 2007–2014. He is past president of the American College Personnel Association and has authored four books and over 50 book chapters and other articles on student affairs, student learning, and leadership.*

SUSAN R. KOMIVES *is professor emerita in the Student Affairs Program at the University of Maryland. She is past president of the Council for the Advancement of Standards in Higher Education, ACPA, and editor of the* Handbook for Student Services *along with other books and articles on student leadership.*

INDEX

ORDER FORM SUBSCRIPTION AND SINGLE ISSUES

DISCOUNTED BACK ISSUES:

Use this form to receive 20% off all back issues of *New Directions for Higher Education*.
All single issues priced at **$23.20** (normally $29.00)

TITLE	ISSUE NO.	ISBN

*Call 1-800-835-6770 or see mailing instructions below. When calling, mention the promotional code JBNND
to receive your discount. For a complete list of issues, please visit www.josseybass.com/go/ndhe*

SUBSCRIPTIONS: (1 YEAR, 4 ISSUES)

☐ New Order ☐ Renewal

U.S.	☐ Individual: $89	☐ Institutional: $335
CANADA/MEXICO	☐ Individual: $89	☐ Institutional: $375
ALL OTHERS	☐ Individual: $113	☐ Institutional: $409

*Call 1-800-835-6770 or see mailing and pricing instructions below.
Online subscriptions are available at www.onlinelibrary.wiley.com*

ORDER TOTALS:

Issue / Subscription Amount: $ _____

Shipping Amount: $ _____
(for single issues only – subscription prices include shipping)

Total Amount: $ _____

SHIPPING CHARGES:	
First Item	$6.00
Each Add'l Item	$2.00

*(No sales tax for U.S. subscriptions. Canadian residents, add GST for subscription orders. Individual rate subscriptions must
be paid by personal check or credit card. Individual rate subscriptions may not be resold as library copies.)*

BILLING & SHIPPING INFORMATION:

☐ **PAYMENT ENCLOSED:** *(U.S. check or money order only. All payments must be in U.S. dollars.)*

☐ **CREDIT CARD:** ☐ VISA ☐ MC ☐ AMEX

Card number _____ Exp. Date _____

Card Holder Name _____ Card Issue # _____

Signature _____ Day Phone _____

☐ **BILL ME:** *(U.S. institutional orders only. Purchase order required.)*

Purchase order # _____
Federal Tax ID 13559302 • GST 89102-8052

Name _____

Address _____

Phone _____ E-mail _____

Copy or detach page and send to: **John Wiley & Sons, One Montgomery Street, Suite 1000,
San Francisco, CA 94104-4594**

Order Form can also be faxed to: **888-481-2665**

PROMO JBNND

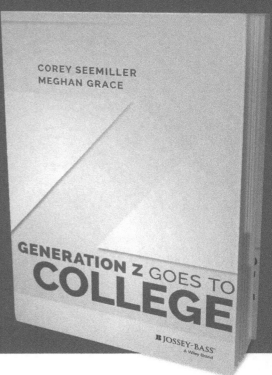